Paula —

my new book

Hope you enjoy it

The View from
Karen's Book Barn

by
Scott Houchin

CARDIAC BOOKS

The book cover and design were created by Lise Neer of Denver, Colorado. Lise also did the beautiful pastel painting on the front cover of the book.

All photos by local La Grange photographer Barbara Manley Calloway.

This book is dedicated to the people of La Grange, Kentucky, my home town. For better or worse, we grew up together and loved each other as we did it.

Contents

PREFACE

I was born and raised in La Grange, Kentucky. Until I was old enough to drive, it was my world. I loved "the town with the tracks running down Main Street." So many times, I was sitting on the school bus when we got to town and there was a train going down Main Street blocking traffic. All of us on the bus knew we would be late for school, but being late for school due to "the train" was part of my town.

I left La Grange when I was still a young man in my early twenties, and for most of the next forty years, I lived at least a thousand miles from the town. Yet, the entire time I was gone, I referred to La Grange as "home". You can take Scott out of Kentucky but you cannot take the Kentucky out of Scott. For me, Kentucky and La Grange are both the same word, "home."

And home I would come. After I retired, I started making regular trips back to La Grange. I frequently found myself doing morning coffee at a place called Karen's Book Barn, which was located right next to the tracks on Main Street. Although, I had been gone for decades, it was a nice surprise to see that this street, which I loved so much, still looked the same as when I was a child. The bank was no longer the bank and the two drugstores were no longer drugstores. The names of the shops had changed but the buildings of my hometown's main street all remained. I would enjoy 'the view" of the buildings of my childhood while drinking my morning coffee at Karen's Book Barn. Sometimes I would go outside in the cool morning before the hot humid days began and just sit by the tracks going down Main Street in the rocking chair someone wisely had put there. Frequently, I would sit for an hour or more remembering why this was home.

And that is why this book exists. Most of the short stories in this book are about the stores and the people that visited those stores in my childhood and high school years. I loved those years and I also loved my hometown.

I hope you enjoy the book.

Chapter 1

Head's Drugs

Head's Drugs — or "Head's" — was located on the Main Street in downtown LA (La Grange, Kentucky, that is). It was right next to the bank and on the north side of the tracks, the same side of the tracks as the La Grange Volunteer Fire Department. When the trains came through town there was still enough room in front of Head's that the newspaper boys had room to unload the bundles of papers and distribute them to each other. I mention this because the train goes down the middle of Main Street and there is not a lot of room for the train, cars, the sidewalk, Head's customers, and the bicycles.

The "paper boys" had all sorts of Big Daddy Roth customized bicycles with front baskets that were huge — large enough to fit 30 or 40 newspapers in. They would have to lean the bikes against buildings because their "load" of newspapers was too heavy for a normal kickstand and the bikes would just fall over. After they loaded the baskets they would get on their bikes and go all over town delivering Louisville's *Courier-Journal*.

I used to go there in the morning and watch them load their bikes. I was jealous. For 12- and 13-year-olds, it was the happening place. Those newspaper delivery boys made real money, at least it seemed like a lot to me. I wanted to be one of them.

In my home town Head's was "The Hub." And my best Head's Drug's story has to do with my father!

Every small town in the South had an F.W. Woolworth's Five and Dime store, including LA and every Five and Dime has a soda fountain but the coolest soda fountain in LA was at Head's. They made the best chocolate milkshakes. We would watch them put in scoop after scoop of ice cream and then all that chocolate! The whole mix was then put into the big aluminum milkshake container and attached to the mixer. That noise! When they finally poured out "The Shake" it moved like thick molasses. It took 30 seconds to fill a 12-oz. glass. Or at least it seemed like 30 seconds to an 8 to 13-year-old kid. It was the best. Because it was LA, everybody knew each other. The woman working the fountain knew who we were; who our parents were; and who our grandparents were. Everybody was on a first-name basis. When I did not feel like a milkshake, I would do a cherry Coke. The next best thing.

After the milkshake I would usually wander to the back of the store where the magazines and comic books were located. Head's had all the regulars: Superman, Batman and Robin, Archie, others. However, my favorite was Sergeant Rock and Easy Company. This was the Fifties and fighting Nazis was not that long ago — barely a decade earlier. So, Sgt. Rock and his squad were the cat's meow.

My mom would drop my sister Pat and me off at Head's and then run errands all over town. Mom knew that between the drinks and my love of reading Sgt. Rock, she did not have to be back to pick us up for a couple of hours. This was what "going to town" meant to me for years, until I started playing football and basketball after school. This changed the routine and after practice I would walk from La Grange Elementary School on Fifth Street to Head's and then call for Mom or Dad to come pick me up. My family lived in the country and it was way too far to walk home. Even bicycling was too far and unthinkable in the winter. By the time I got out of football or basketball practice in the winter, it was getting dark. So,

I would walk to Head's and call Mom or Dad to be picked up.

And that is when it happened!

One day after practice, I walked to Head's and asked if I could use the phone. My family had a deal with Head's and I was allowed to use their phone, but I was taught to ask permission first. There were two reasons for this. The first reason is that I am from the South, where you say "Yes ma'am" and "Yes sir"; hold the door open for women (of all ages) — and men too for that matter — and when you use the phone at someone else's house you ask permission first. The second reason is: Head's Drugs was one of only two drugstores in town, and people needed medicine from Head's for their medical conditions, so the phone line needed to be open for patients' calls. That is what I was told. And being from the South, I did not question what my parents told me.

Back to my story:

One day I walked into Head's Drugs with all my books, football gear, etc. and asked if I could use the phone. "Sure," was the answer. I walked to the phone, which was about ten feet from the soda counter, and picked up the receiver. But something was wrong. There was no dial tone — or anything! I pressed a "2" button on the phone (as I remember — the phone did not have a dial but had buttons) and it made a "beep." Then I heard someone on the other end say, "Is this Billy"? Billy was Mr. Head's first name — the voice was asking for Billy Head. I also recognized the voice. It was my dad.

A little explanation for those that do not know: My dad was one of two doctors in town and he sometimes called in prescriptions. Usually his nurse called in the prescriptions but sometimes he did, which was the case that day.

As bored kids, my friends and I had sometimes talked about the probability that one of us would pick up a phone to call someone and at that exact same moment the person on the other end would be calling that phone at the very same time. Thus, the phone did not ring or anything. You would just pick up the phone and another person would be there! It seemed pretty "far out" to me at the time and I never really thought than it would ever happen to me. Not only did it happen to me but it happened with my own dad on Billy Head's phone! This was beyond cool.

It being my dad, though, of course when I said, "Dad, is that you?" he simply responded, "This is Doctor Houchin. Is Billy there"? And when I replied, "Dad, this is Scott —

your son," and was about to comment on how absolutely bizarre I thought it was for me to pick up the phone at Head's Drugs and find my own father on the other end of the phone at the exact same moment!! He simply said, "Scott?" And when I said "yes " it being my dad, he said, "Put Billy on the phone. I need to call in a prescription."

While I was having "a moment" that I would remember some 50 years later, all my dad said was, "Put Billy on the phone." It was as if this happened not just every day but two or three times per day. As if it were a totally normal occurrence.

Rather than write another five thousand words on my relationship with my dad, I will just say that this story is pretty typical. I, being Scott, and he, being Dr. Houchin. That simple conversation in that particular situation is exactly the story of our relationship.

I went and got Billy Head and put him on the phone.

The next day at school I did talk it up with several other kids and they just kind of went "Duh". They were not really polite about it. As kids, we were frequently not very polite to each other. As they say in medicine, the event was "unremarkable" to the kids and I never brought it up again. The event was kind of remarkable to me though, and I remember it now, over fifty years later.

When I got my driver's license the after-school scene changed. Many times, we (the gang) went to Joe's Big O, but still on weekends or on those days when I did not have school or work, it was nice to go to Head's and do a milkshake. I had also progressed from Sergeant Rock comics to Playboy. As I remember it, if you knew where to look in the magazine section you could usually find Playboy or something like it. Thus, a milkshake and some "literature".

I graduated from Oldham County High School in 1969 and I believe it was that same year that tragedy came to LA. One of our boys had been killed in Vietnam. His mother worked at Head's. I will not use names out of respect for all concerned, but for those that do know the players I am sure you remember.

The mother had been very nice, a welcome sight at Head's. She always seemed cheerful, and when we kids acted up, which was frequently, she would "handle" any situations we threw her way with a little bit of discipline but mostly understanding. Sometimes we were brats but we all liked the mother.

Anyway, the word came down that her son had been killed in Vietnam. He was at least two years — possibly three years — my senior, so I didn't really know him that well. I knew her much better than her son. Still, he was one of our LA boys. Everybody in town knew who he was and regretted what had happened. As a town we grieved and tried to console the mother. It was very hard. I do not believe I have ever met anyone that looked so hurt. When she returned to work, it was obvious that she was trying as hard as she could, but she had simply been injured too deeply by the death of her son to recover. I was just a high school dumbass kid but when I saw her at Head's I always felt her pain. It was obvious that she had a tremendous amount of pain. "Wounded" is the word that comes to mind. She did not act like she was wounded. She was wounded. Deeply, and to my knowledge she probably did not ever fully recover from losing her son.

Thus, in a way, Head's became just like the rest of America. The war had come home to LA. Tragedy in a small town, and the entire town felt the pain.

I went to college after that and my visits to Head's decreased. I moved away to Gatlinburg, Tennessee for a while; then went back to the University of Louisville off and on into the mid-Seventies; then moved to Boulder, CO; then to Boston; and then to Denver. However, I never forgot about Head's.

And there's a reason for that. It's the name: Head's Drugs. Yes, this was the end of the Sixties and the beginning of the Seventies, and the word "head" at that time had numerous meanings: "Pot head." "He is a head" — a hippie. As with many terms in that era, the word "head" started meaning whatever you wanted it to.

Wherever I lived, I'd find a way to bring up something about my hometown drugstore — "Head's Drugs." I'd almost instantly get the reaction I expected. "Really? Your hometown has a Drugstore called Head's Drugs?" Then I'd get to explain that, really, we did. The other amazing thing that I told people about my hometown LA was that a train ran down the middle of the town. And it still does.

It did not matter if I was talking to Harvard types in Boston or ski and/or bicycle bums in Colorado: Two things that almost always brought a smile to folks' faces were Head's Drugs and the train that went down the main street of my hometown.

And it still does. Most people simply did not believe me. I mean, who has a train running down the main street of their hometown? Maybe an interstate like in Vail, but a train?

The train that runs down Main Street is one of the reasons LA has become such a tourist attraction. LA takes its tourism seriously, with committees set up to keep the town historical and "picturesque." Perhaps we should find the ole "Head's Drugs" sign and put it back up to bring in more tourists. It couldn't hurt.

As I remember it, everybody loved Head's Drugs. It was a town hub. A place to catch the latest on what was going on in LA. It was a part of LA that we all remember and miss.

Chapter 2

Donnie – A Family Affair

I knew Donnie almost from birth. We both went to kindergarten together. Our first day of kindergarten was my first clue that something was wrong. All of us kiddies were a little shook up with our first day of "school." However, Donnie completely fell apart. He literally had a breakdown of sorts. He cried, deeply, hysterically. It was unclear exactly what was wrong. He could not talk because he was crying too hard. He was making such a spectacle that the teacher and some of the mothers had to take him outside, and he did not come back that day.

The rest of us kids were scared, slightly confused, feeling some anticipation, but mostly having fun. Being in a room with all the kids on the block and some from other blocks was new and different. For most of us the fun aspect quickly took over and we were enjoying ourselves. Donnie went home crying.

Later, when I asked my mother about it, she downplayed it to the point that I never brought it up again. The other kids did remember it. At our fortieth high school reunion, I mentioned this event to a classmate who was in our kindergarten class. She remembered it clearly. We were not sure what was going on, but the incident is such that I can remember it vividly 60 years later, like it was yesterday. It is my biggest — and almost only — memory of kindergarten.

The best word that I can think of to describe Donnie is "fragile." The basis for his condition was never revealed to me. To this day, I still do not understand what his living situation was. For as long as I can remember, he lived with his father. For most of my life, I thought his father was his uncle and that he lived with his uncle. Only in researching this story did I find out that the person I thought was his uncle was his father. I never knew what happened to his mother and, for some reason, even as a young adult I was never informed as to what exactly his family situation was. Apparently, his family life was not explained to children, and being from the South, I did not ask.

Donnie was a town project. His status as "fragile" could be sensed almost immediately. Our town was a small, rural farm town in the South and too soon we all started realizing that there was something going on with Donnie. In many ways he was just like the rest of us, but underneath all of that, we knew something was wrong.

Whatever it was, he was just an arm's length from falling apart and we knew it.

The small, rural farm town I grew up in is La Grange, Kentucky or "LA" as we called it, had its standard-issue bullies like every other town in America. However, Donnie was never picked on by bullies. Under normal circumstances he would be the exact person picked on by an asshole bully. Good-natured, smart, and tall but not that fit, nonathletic. He would be perceived as weak. However, it was never spoken, and it was never written, but it was known by all that if anyone ever picked on Donnie the rest of us would come to his defense. Immediately! Donnie's status was something that I certainly did not have. When bullies picked on me, I was on my own. Like I said, it was never stated out loud but if anyone ever started pushing Donnie around or making rude comments to him, we would all rally to his aid immediately. Looking out for Donnie was a family affair in LA. I'm not sure folks from outside the family — that is, outside our town — would ever understand, but that's the way it was.

I got to know Donnie well for two reasons. First, my last name is Houchin and Donnie's last name is Ireland,

and in school we sat alphabetically, so in every class we shared, Donnie sat behind me. Second, my mother, who had been there that first day of kindergarten when Donnie had his meltdown, had asked me to keep an eye on Donnie so that other kids would not pick on him. So, at an early age I started paying attention to Donnie. And in no time, there was a connection. We became pals.

Not all the time. I played with the cool kids as much as they would let me. Donnie was neither cool nor athletic. I believe the big deal back then was skateboarding and twist contests. I doubt that Donnie ever got on a skateboard or ever danced the twist his entire life. But I did.

I tried to fit in with the cool kids. They lived in town. I lived out in the country, a couple of miles out from LA, and I was only allowed to ride my bike into town one or two days a week in the summer. So, when all the cool kids were skateboarding, swimming, playing baseball, basketball, football, dancing — basically being kids — I would try to bike into town as often as I could to be social. Girls! Yes, going to town was "Where the Girls Are" among the cool kids. The entire social structure of our small town as kids revolved around hanging with "the gang," and I tried hard to fit in.

Donnie did none of the cool kid things.

Donnie liked to read. So, did I! Books were our pals. It was part of the connection. Donnie was smart! We would chat about books before and after class, and sometimes exchange them. One of the favorites back in those days was Up Periscope, a WWII thriller that was later made into a movie starring James Garner. Lots of guys walked around our high school freshman year with Up Periscope in their back pockets, including Donnie and me. We also read books that were not about WWII. Everything from the Hardy Boys to Steinbeck. We loaned each other books and talked about books. I cannot remember seeing Donnie when he did not have a book — a non-schoolbook — with him. As we moved up in grades, the books we shared got better.

High school meant a whole new crowd to hang with. Kids from Crestwood, Pewee Valley, Liberty and over on the highway (US 42). Still Donnie was sitting behind me in homeroom and other classes — Mrs. Jenkins' English class, Miss Adams' Homeroom, and Dutch Holland's Lit class. We kept our connection all through high school.

And then, I started driving and I found out about beer, smoking cigarettes, and girls. Donnie passed on all of those.

For folks who did not know him, probably a good question would be: was Donnie gay? Back in those days, what I have described would sound like someone who might be gay. Back in the Fifties, any male who seemed "different" in any way was viewed as "possibly gay". Back then being considered gay was, literally, dangerous. Gay guys were open game, getting beaten up all the time. As homophobic and sick as that may sound, this was the South and our schools had just become integrated. When I started grade school, the school for the African American kids and the schools for "white folks" were two different schools — something called separate-but-equal, which was complete and total bullshit. I'm describing segregated schools to paint a picture of the times and to remind readers how folks reacted to gay boys and men. It was ignorance at its worst. In a small rural farm town in the South in the Fifties and early Sixties, no one wanted to be gay. Better said, no one wanted others to know they were gay because it was so dangerous.

Something was wrong with Donnie, but it was not that. I never saw him with a girl — or guy —holding hands! Ever! I am pretty sure he was into girls. In fact, we used to talk about girls. However, he was way too shy. He never asked any girls out. Whatever it was with Donnie, it did not let him get close to women — or anyone else — romantically. To my knowledge he never had a girlfriend the entire time I knew him, which was most of his life.

We graduated from Oldham County High School, Class of '69. I seem to remember a photo my mother took of Donnie and me in our graduation gowns. However, there were a lot of photos that day.

I did not see Donnie most of that summer. However, we both decided to go to the same college the next year, Georgetown College in Georgetown, Ky. As I remember, he may have received some sort of scholarship — probably something Reverend Meacham might have helped him get. Everybody in town was on Donnie's side, trying to help him out.

About me going to Georgetown: I had absolutely no business going to college. I was very immature for my age and I really should have waited a couple of years before going to college to let myself do a little growing up.

Unfortunately, there was this thing called the Vietnam War and if you were an 18-year-old male and you did not go to college (a "2S deferment") then you were drafted and quite possibly would go to Vietnam. So, I went to college, a place I shouldn't have been at that time. Why did I choose a place called Georgetown College in Georgetown, Ky.? A friend of mine told me about Georgetown and I decided to go there.

When I heard that Donnie was going there as well, I offered to drive him up to college. It was a great ride to Georgetown! It was a new adventure — both of us going off to college! I believe our stuff was already in our dorms because we had taken it a week earlier, but this was a Sunday afternoon and classes started the next day on Monday. So, we went up together. A cool ride. Kind of like sitting in homeroom people-watching, replaced by backroad scenery driving to Shelbyville on Hwy. 53 and then on to Georgetown from I-64. Good day. I still remember it over forty years later.

My first year of college I was a serious student. I think I maintained over a 3-point average, mostly because I was just scared to death about going to college, and because my mother and sister were constantly on my butt about my grades that first year. But by Year Two I knew the drill, so I started having fun, and I had way too much fun. A spoiled, white, middle-class, dumbass living in a dorm with free meals. My grades suffered significantly. I learned how to study just enough to get by with a C — or 2-point average. Just enough to stay out of the war. I had friends at school who did not keep their average above a 2-point and they were drafted, and they did go to Vietnam. However, that is another story.

I would see Donnie around campus. Mostly at breakfast. Georgetown is small, and all the students ate at the same cafeteria. Usually he was eating alone. I had a girlfriend by that time and I usually ate with her and/or her friends and/or my drinking buddies. I would always make it a point to say howdy to Donnie when I saw him and, in some ways, it was just like our high school years. Sometimes I would see him with a small group of pals he'd made. But too many times I'd see Donnie eating alone or sitting in the TV room of his dorm, watching TV by himself on a Saturday night.

I left Georgetown. Better stated, I left Georgetown and did not look back. It was the times. The Vietnam War, the draft, Kent State, those were hard times in many ways in America.

By accident, I found out about a way to avoid the draft. It is a very long story in itself. However, basically it comes down to this: If you were a student and you dropped your 2S deferment, you became draft eligible. If you were not drafted within the next 3 months, you were out of the draft due to a loophole. Vietnam was never a declared war. Thus, technically, and legally, we (America) were in peacetime. During peacetime if you were not drafted within three months of becoming 1A then you could not be drafted unless there was a declared war.

As stated, Vietnam was never a declared war. The United States held a press conference and stated that there would be no draftees for the next 6 months. So, the War Resisters League did the math and its research of the laws and went public telling all students that wanted out of the war to drop their 2S deferment and hopefully – you would get out!

I dropped my 2S deferment. I drank myself to sleep almost every night. I was a complete wreck and I sweated blood for 3 months and then I was out! They sent me a letter stating that I would not be draft eligible unless there was a war (declared and legal war). I quit Georgetown College the day after getting out of the draft and I did not look back.

I did tell Donnie about this way out of the draft. I did not realize it then but probably he would never have been drafted anyway. However, I did go to his dorm room and tell him about it. In fact, I told just about all my friends this way out of the draft.

About two weeks after I got out of the draft and quit college, I hitchhiked to Gatlinburg, Tennessee with a good buddy. I lived there for the next several years. I was waiting tables in Gatlinburg and made pretty good money. This combined with meeting kids from all over the South and playing music together was an amazingly happy time. Finally, I was in the place I should have been all along instead of going to college.

While I was playing hippie down in Gatlinburg, Donnie graduated from Georgetown College and he moved back to LA, but I never heard that he got a job of any sort.

After I'd been waiting tables for a couple of years, I finally realized why I needed to get a college education. I believe back then in the south we called it "finding out the meaning of a dollar." I moved back to LA to go to the

University of Louisville. I started going to school full time in order to "get that piece of paper" aka a Bachelor's degree. I started out living with my folks during this time, but eventually I got tired of the commute and moved into Louisville, where I was a student until I graduated.

During that 1973-74 time when I was living at my parents' house, I would hang with some of my high school pals and often on the weekends, with no classes the following day, we would go in to Louisville. At that time LA and Oldham County were "dry" -- you couldn't buy alcohol -- so we would haunt the bars in Louisville. Our favorites were on Washington Street next to the Second Street Bridge, at the Butchertown Pub, and bars on Bardstown Road. There were no "drinking and driving" laws back then, so frequently on those jaunts we would not return to LA until late at night or early the next morning. Back then, LA was still a very small town. I-71 was open, but school busing for desegregation in Jefferson County had not gone into effect yet and the massive white flight from Louisville had not happened. It was not until the second half of the Seventies that the population explosion started when thousands of whites fleeing busing left Louisville and relocated in Oldham County.

On those hot, steamy, summer nights, at 1 a.m. in the morning, we would drive into LA and stop at the 4-way stop at the tracks. There was always a cop car sitting on the corner, so we always had to stop at the sign instead of just running it. Too many times when we momentarily stopped at the 4-way stop, we would see someone walking the streets in those early morning hours. We immediately recognized the walk as Donnie's "get along" — sort of a bouncy walk that was his trademark.

Someone would always say, "Is that Donnie?" and all of us would look and confirm that it was indeed Donnie, walking, bouncing down the street at 1 a.m. in the morning, by himself. All of us in the car were thinking the same thing: "What amount of loneliness and anguish would bring Donnie out of his bed to be walking the streets of LA, by himself, in the early hours of the morning?"

It was possible that we had it completely wrong. For all I know, Donnie had joined Jane Fonda's workout program and was doing cardio training. Her program was popular back then and it was summer in Kentucky, which redefines the words "hot and humid." Perhaps he was working out and doing it late at night simply because it was cooler at 1 in the morning than 1 in the afternoon. Wishful thinking. On other trips, we saw Donnie walking in those early morning hours in the middle of December, which kind of kills the workout theory. I will never know, but what I do know is that when I saw him bouncing down the streets of LA early in the morning, I instantly flashed on his first day of kindergarten. In my mind I said the words, "Something is wrong."

Some will say, "Well, if you realized something was wrong, why didn't you do something about it?"

There was a reason.

LA in the early Seventies was like much of the country. It was still torn by years of bitter protest and opposition. True, the demonstrations had not happened in La Grange, but Oldham County and La Grange had young men who were killed in Vietnam, and there were men in Oldham County and LA who had "beaten the draft" — and I was one of them. There is a long list of social and political situations where LA was pulled out of the 1950s and dropped into the 1970s. A hornet's nest of conflict, and no time to adjust. It was not an easy time in LA, nor was it an easy time in America. It was also not an easy time for me.

Many of the people I'd loved growing up now looked at me as "one of them"— the people who were against the war, who'd gotten out of the war, and were now — the nice version — "civil rights workers." There were other names they called us.

And although in many ways we all still loved each other, in many ways we were working for separate and different Americas. It was hard. Very hard. The sense of betrayal, disillusion, fear, and anger that swept the country was felt loud and clear in LA

I could not really do anything for Donnie after I got out of the draft simply because I was having a hard-enough time just taking care of myself, and having only moderate success. I was living at my parents' house. Dead broke. Going to school. Disillusioned and beaten down from what was going on in America. I had been raised to be red, white, and blue, and to have lifelong family friends suddenly saying I, and people like me, were the problem was very hard to digest. Of course, they were wrong, but some of these people had been my family's friends since my birth. As many of my generation said, we felt like we were the true heroes of America by stopping an injustice to the people of Vietnam as well as the hundreds of thousands of American young men and women being sent there. The wounds of that era have still not healed and I am reluctant to write about it because it is still raw over a half a century later.

So, although I saw Donnie walking, alone, in the middle of the night, I did not contact him regarding his behavior. I did mention it to my Dad at times. After all, he was the town doctor. He usually told me that there was probably nothing that I could do, which was true. We had all been trying to help Donnie for the last 20 years. If Donnie was going to make it, it was up to Donnie to do it. Apparently, he was making moves in that direction.

He was learning to drive. In a town like LA, for a grown man to not have a car to drive around town was socially the kiss of death. The entire social structure of a place like LA depended upon your ability to move around and of course there is that thing called money. Without a car, a job would be hard to find in a small, rural, farm town in the South. Basically, Donnie was a fish out of water. If Donnie ever hoped to find a job — and a girlfriend, a wife, a life — he had to learn to drive.

Apparently, Donnie realized this and was taking steps to get his license. Maybe he actually did get his driver's license. I do not know, but it is obvious that he was taking major steps to improve his life. Good for him!

But then, bad luck.

One Kentucky morning Donnie backed his — or his father's — car into someone else's car. A fender bender. But rather than stick around and do the insurance thing and maybe get a ticket, Donnie just drove off and went back home. Maybe he did not have insurance. Maybe he did not have a license. It does not matter. He left the scene of an auto accident, and even if it was just a fender bender, leaving the scene of an auto accident and going home, was a mistake, a bad mistake. Illegal.

I suspect the same Donnie who broke down his first day of kindergarten was the same Donnie who made the decision to go home after the fender bender. Home was a safe place and he wanted to be in it.

The story I got was this: the other car's owner wrote down Donnie's license plate number and called the police. They ran the plates, and one of my childhood friends, now a policeman, was given the job of visiting Donnie. I don't know if Donnie was being arrested or what. The story I got was that Donnie said he wanted to go get his hat which he had left in his bedroom. So, my friend let him go get his hat. Somewhere on that trip to his bedroom he located a gun and he shot himself. Killed himself.

That is what my father told me. There was never any reason to question the story. I distinctly remember I was at home at the kitchen table studying for a test at U of L when Dad walked in saying he had some bad news, and then he told me the story.

About the actual suicide: you do not have to be a screenwriter to fill in the blanks on this. My guess is that he knew the police would be coming, so he located the gun. Obviously, someone had a gun in the house. His gun or his dad's gun. I don't know.

Personally, I cannot imagine Donnie buying a gun, although back then you didn't need a license to buy a gun on Main Street in LA. I do not know if he used a pistol or a shotgun or a rifle. I think Donnie was probably hoping they would not come for him, but when they did, it was too much for him and he pulled the trigger.

No words.

Just as we had always done, the town rallied in support of Donnie. Many of the same boys, now young men, guys who would have protected Donnie if a bully picked on him, were now his pallbearers. I was one of them.

We buried Donnie. I do not remember much about the funeral or the ceremony at the gravesite, which is odd. Usually, as a writer/detail sort of guy, I would remember the details. I believe the whole thing was just too painful for me to remember. Donnie was not the first of my classmates who I'd buried, but I was closer to him than any other classmate I'd buried up to that time.

I have heard from friends that some folks say they did not know about the suicide until they saw Donnie's father out in the front yard of his house wailing with pain and grief.

Donnie killed himself in 1975. I graduated from U of L in 1976 and moved to Boulder, Colorado a week after graduating.

I suspect my last conversation with Donnie took place at Georgetown College when I walked over to his dorm after I found out I was out of the draft and I was preparing to leave Georgetown. I know I did go to several professors and explain to them why I was leaving and I believe I also let Donnie know that I was leaving. I don't remember specifically doing it but I think I did. However, I do remember seeing him in his dorm. Numerous times. I would walk in and find him watching TV. It did not matter what time of day it was. In all G-town dorms there was a TV area right on the first floor, with couches, chairs, tables. I'd walk into the dorm and see him immediately. I always said "hello" to him, and he always said "hello" back.

I think of Donnie probably too often. Back when I was a hippie, I tried to write a song about him but was totally unsuccessful. Now, over 40 years after his death, I have started writing and finally can tell Donnie's story as I know it.

.

I am writing this while visiting Kentucky. Oddly enough, I just heard a song on WAKY (yes, the radio station is still around) and instantly thought of him. It's the song about Vincent Van Gogh by Don McLean — "Starry Starry Night." Donnie was no Vincent Van Gogh but there are similarities. Donnie was a lonely guy. He was my pal.

Now, when I come back to Kentucky to be a medic on bicycle rides, I always visit LA at least once each trip. I would really have enjoyed walking into one of the local coffee places on Main Street in LA— Karen's Book Barn, Coffee Roaster's, and seeing Donnie, maybe with his wife. Even better, his wife and kids! See him having a morning coffee with his wife and kids. Wow! If he'd gotten the car thing down and finally found a job and gotten involved in the social thing in LA, he might have found a wife.... Looking from the outside, it looked like he was taking steps in that direction.

He didn't make it.

Donnie, you were my friend and you are missed.

Donnie died in 1975, but his gravestone does not have the date. He is buried at the Valley of Rest Cemetery in La Grange.

Chapter 3

Gene Armstrong

He was the father of my best friend. Gene Armstrong, father of Tom Armstrong, who was part of our gang of "best friends" or, as the millennials say, BFFs. For many years Gene was simply Tom's dad — an old guy I'd say "hello" to as we gathered every night to go out and do the kind of stuff kids do in high school.

We picked up Tom at his house and his dad was usually sitting there watching TV. We would say hello and chitchat a little, then leave. Gene always called me "Doc", which I liked very much. Of course, he called me that because my dad was one of our town's doctors, but no other adult called me "Doc." My classmates called me "Doc," but Gene Armstrong was the only adult who did. I noticed it and liked it. It was one of the reasons I liked him.

Gene was the town reporter and sometimes-editor of the local newspaper, *The Oldham Era*. The paper was an institution in my small rural farm town in the South. Football games, yard sales, church events, weddings: everything that happened in town was in *The Oldham Era*. It came out once a week. It was printed over in

Simpsonville in Shelby County, about 25 miles down Hwy. 53.

After Tom got his driver's license, he got the job of driving the paper over to be printed, and, given that I was a high school kid always looking for a chance to get out of the house, I volunteered to go assist him. Sometimes he would just pick me up because I lived "on the way" on Hwy. 53, but most times I'd drive to his house and we'd go down to the newspaper office on the corner of Walnut and Main Street in downtown LA to pick up the sheets to be printed. Because we were doing "official *Era* business" we could walk past the front desk and back into the actual heart of the operation, which seemed special to me. The inks and all the various machines — mechanical movement everywhere in the room — strange machines — nothing like I had ever seen before. Certainly nothing like I had seen at school or in a Doctor's office. And then there was the desk where they put the actual paper together. I always enjoyed going there and seeing the guts of publishing the written word.

At the *Era* office, Gene was very busy. He was obviously in charge. Ordering changes – reviewing this and that –more changes. He seemed like a different person than the man I knew as Tom's dad sitting around watching TV at home, relaxing with a beer in his hand and looking up at me and saying, "How's it going Doc

The Marble Hill Nuclear Power Plant was being built in Madison, Indiana. I became one of the Kentucky organizers opposing it. A half dozen of us did a walk from Louisville to Madison, Indiana to raise awareness on the Kentucky side of the river. We started the walk on the Belvedere in downtown Louisville, and the second night we stopped in La Grange. I saw Gene at the Oldham County Courthouse as we walked into town and settled in for the night. He had his son John with him, and we chatted for a bit and discussed Marble Hill. "Keep it up, Doc," he said as we parted. I took that as a sign from Gene that I'd "done good"; that instead of being a dumb immature high school kid, I was now someone to be taken seriously; that I'd "made it" and our group was doing something good for LA That's how I interpreted it. I still remember his words now more than 35 years later.

Nuclear war and nuclear power are complex subjects. I will make this as short as possible. At that time, we were in the middle of the Cold War. From that time on, nuclear power plants have been first-strike targets in military or terrorist attacks. In the late Seventies most people did not realize this, but I did, and so did the people I was walking to Madison with. If there was any sort of nuclear confrontation, I was all too aware that my hometown was barely 20 miles from Marble Hill, which would be a first-strike target because of its nuclear power plant. It would be hit first: before Fort Knox with all its gold, before Louisville, before anywhere else within hundreds of miles. Functioning nuclear power plants are first-strike targets.

I personally did not think that any elected official or any country leader would intentionally "push the button." My primary concern was that there'd be a malfunction in the system, or even worse, that an airplane pilot who wanted to commit suicide or a terrorist group that had taken over a plane would crash it into an active nuke plant.

This was pre - 9/11. They used to refer to us as "nut cases" when we talked about a terrorist group seizing a plane and crashing into a nuclear plant. Now, of course, this is a major concern throughout the whole world. But back then the folks running nuclear power plants said this kind of thing would never happen, and even if it did, the nuclear containment building would keep anything serious from happening.

These are the same folks that designed the nuclear power plant in Fukushima, Japan, that fell victim to an earthquake and tsunami. The same folks who assured all concerned that a threat from an earthquake and tsunami was not possible. Today the Fukushima nuclear power plant is continuing to meltdown, contaminating the entire northern Pacific with radioactive material. This has been going on for years. The Japanese authorities still do not know what they are going to do to stop the ongoing meltdown. This blind arrogance regarding nature reminds me of the people that built the Titanic. The ship that could not sink – but it did.

We knew we had to stop the Marble Hill nuclear plant. Our walk aimed to educate the locals along U.S. 42 and in LA about the danger they were in.

There was nothing remarkable about seeing Gene and John when we walked into LA but it is something I remember even now, years later.

Non-violent political direct action was not something that folks in LA were used to, but this small rural farm town in the South responded well. A fair number of folks came out and showed their support and treated us well.

We stopped Marble Hill.

A few years later I was working at the Kentucky Commission on Human Rights in Louisville. One day I received a phone call from my dad, the local doctor in LA. He said that Gene had been in a car wreck and was at Louisville's General Hospital. The Commission was only a 10-minute drive from the hospital. My father asked if I could go visit Gene.

When a local from LA is in the hospital in Louisville and you are in the area, you visit them. It really doesn't matter whether you're close to the person or not. If someone from LA is in the hospital you go visit. My dad expected me to visit Gene, and it didn't even enter my mind that I wouldn't. It was how I was raised.

He was in General Hospital for over a week.

When I got to General, I felt like I was walking into a ward in a hospital in London during the Blitz. Beds were closer to being cots than actual beds. They had none of the electric devices to lower and raise the mattresses. They were just simple beds with clean white sheets in a room with 5 to 10 other beds — a ward.

It was late morning and it was a long way from LA so Gene did not have any visitors. It was just him and me. For the first time in our lives, we talked without other people around. To my surprise, we connected. I don't remember all the details of his accident, but he told me he'd gone off the road and that a second vehicle was not involved. He was hurt but I do not think he had major injuries. I believe he was just there for observation. When a patient Gene's age — he was in his late 50s or older — had a traumatic incident back then, they would keep them in the hospital for observation. This was 1981. This was before the days when patient care was determined by insurance companies. This was back in the days when a doctor said "keep the patient in the hospital for observation," and that was enough. The present is obviously, a different era. Now he probably would have been released after the first night.

I went back to visit Gene at least twice before he was released from the hospital.

Shortly after that I moved to Boston and I did not see him for a couple of years.

I next saw Gene at Tom's wedding. It was a beautiful wedding, by the rocky beaches of southern Maine in Wells/Kennebunk Maine, one of my favorite places on earth. The first time I was in Maine had been on a bicycle pilgrimage in New England. I had already visited Martha's Vineyard, the Cape, and biked in Vermont. I'd ridden over to Portsmouth, New Hampshire and camped in Wells, Maine. I'd contacted Tom Armstrong and his girlfriend, Brenda, prior to that trip and arranged to spend my last week with them before heading back to Louisville. The theory being that after a couple of weeks on the road sleeping in tents, on the ground, or in hostels, a warm, clean, comfortable bed with friends around would be just what the doctor ordered.

Tom and Brenda picked me up at the small bar in Wells where we had agreed to meet. As we drove up the road to their house, I found myself speechless. I had only seen places like this in the movies. That people I actually knew lived in such a beautiful place was a little hard to grasp. It turned out that Brenda's family owned this beautiful piece of property on the cliffs of Wells, Maine. The thundering waves of the Atlantic Ocean were pounding on the rocky ledges not 250 feet from their house when we drove up. I instantly thought of the movie A Summer Place, where

Tab Hunter makes it with some hot debutante. The setting for that movie was probably Monterey, California but this was just as spellbindingly beautiful. And I was going to be staying there for a couple of nights! Excellent! The place became one of my all-time favorite places on earth.

Now Tom and Brenda were getting married there, and the whole Armstrong clan had come up to Maine.

By now this was my neck of the woods. I had been living in Boston for six or seven years, and it was really nice to have one of my favorite families from my past up here visiting and having a celebration. The only bad news was that Gene was getting old. He looked old. The last time I had seen Gene was when I visited him in General Hospital and now, he used a walker or wheelchair to get around. Although it had only been a few years since I had last seen him, he looked 20 years older.

I really did not have a chance to talk to him much. After all, he was the father of the groom and the center of much attention. However, on that trip I learned something about Gene I'd never known before: he had been in the Cocoanut Grove Nightclub the night it burned down in 1942. Or he had been there the night before. I never got the story straight on that. In 1942 Gene was in the Navy —

it was during WW II — on leave in Boston, and had gone to the Cocoanut Grove, which was a hot spot back in those days. The Cocoanut Grove Fire was one of the worst restaurant fires in America. Almost 500 people died. The Cocoanut Grove restaurant was in Boston and we were staying in Southern Maine. A New England tragedy and Gene was part of it — a part of New England history. It was all "very New England," which matters up there. It was something everyone could talk to the father of the groom about and it was a source of conversation for everyone. Two families were coming together for a wedding and both families found a story that brought them together. We all enjoyed hearing about Gene's colorful life.

The wedding went off without a hitch on a beautiful sunny day next to the crashing waves of the Atlantic Ocean. And that was the last time I saw Gene.

A few years later after I moved to Colorado, I was sitting at my desk in Denver when I got the call that Gene had died. The news hit me like a rock. I'm not sure why I was so surprised. I had not lived in Kentucky for well over a decade, yet I seemed to think my friends and family in LA would live forever. I am a dreamer!

Gene was someone I'd liked and respected. He was a part of my childhood and adolescence; part of what shaped me as a person. He was an authentic hero — but not just to me.

LA has had a lot of heroes, but none stand out like Gene and what he did. Of course, a major component of being a hero is being at the right place at the right time — which Gene was — but there's more to being a hero. In a life-threatening situation, a hero knows what to do and does it. Gene knew, and he acted.

The Hero

Gene loved to fish. The Ohio River was too far away for an afternoon fishing trip after work, and to be quite honest about it, in 1963 almost no one ate anything they caught in the Ohio River. Louisville and La Grange were downriver from Pittsburg and Cincinnati. You do not have to be a weatherman to know which way the sewage flows, to paraphrase Bob Dylan. Eating anything that came out of the Ohio River was considered dangerous.

Gene would go fishing at Cash's Lake, about four miles south on Hwy. 53 from downtown LA It was close enough to town for an afternoon of fishing after work while relaxing with a couple of beers. Kind of what the American Dream was back then.

Cash's Lake was a country club, golf course and swimming pool. The "lake" was really a series of small lakes, popular with locals because they were easy to get to and had great facilities — (bathrooms, changing rooms). The swimming pool was the best around and it was a country club. It was a great place to go.

I imagine Gene went there on a Wednesday afternoon in May because it was spring in Kentucky. The Derby had been a couple of weeks earlier. Kentucky is beautiful that time of year. Since it was a Wednesday, I expect Gene had just put the paper to bed — that is, the paper had gone to the printer and his job was done. He could rest, grab a few beers, hop in the car, and take it easy by going fishing a couple of miles down the road, enjoy life. Which is exactly what he did.

At some point a family pulled up across the lake and put their fishing boat into the water. I have heard but cannot verify that it was a newish boat, that it might have been the first time they had used it. The whole family showed up: kids, Grandma, Mom and Dad — the whole bunch of them trying out the boat.

According to the locals, they had a very large outboard motor on that fishing boat and the whole family loaded into the boat and they did not have life preservers. This was not all that uncommon in the Sixties. Life preserver requirements were similar to laws for seat belts in cars, helmets for skiers, helmets for motorcyclist, airbags. These laws all came later after a decade of Ralph Nader and "Nader's Raiders" and the great work they did suing everybody they could sue in corporate America to make life a little safer for the rest of us. I lost a few of my high school classmates to auto accidents because they were not buckled up. It was the way everyone used to ride back then. Thank you, Ralph!

The family started doing laps around the lake. What I heard was that it did not take long before the wake — a large wake due to the loaded-down boat and the fast outboard in the small lake — swamped the boat in the middle of the lake. It sank, quickly, with everyone going into the water.

Gene saw this happening and went into action. Here's Gene's own account of the accident in *The Oldham Era*:

> I arrived at the lake about 4:30 and started fishing on the east side of the lake near the dam. About 5:30 Jim Shannon

arrived by himself and put the boat in the water on the west side of the lake and rode around the lake for about 10 or 15 minutes.

Shannon then crossed the lake to his home and docked the boat where he picked up his family. In another 10-or 15-minutes Jerry Ormes and his family arrived and evidently got into the boat, although I did not see it happen.

Shortly thereafter I heard screams for help and started running across the dam in the direction of where I had last heard the boat and the screams. Upon arriving across the lake, I saw Jerry Ormes walking out of the water and I shouted to him asking what I could do. Orme's replied, 'Go get the old boat'.

I recalled having passed a fishing boat on the east side of the lake and ran back across the dam to the boat. I jumped in the boat only to find it about half full of water. Turning the boat over to empty it required additional time and by the time I had the boat back in the water Ormes jumped in with me.

I rowed Ormes and myself across the lake and tried to question him about the situation at the scene of the accident. Ormes said his mother was dead and he was afraid his little boy was too. When I asked about Jim Shannon and his wife, he said he hadn't seen them.

Upon arriving at the scene, I picked up the Ormes' 14-month-old child and Ormes picked up Ida Shannon and I rowed them to shore; handing Orme's his son, I then returned to the overturned boat and picked up Jerry's wife, Sally, and

Darlene Shannon. Mrs. Ormes had been holding onto the two young Shannon children, keeping them from drowning.

When we reached shore, it was evident that no one else at the scene could be helped and Ormes got his wife, child, and the two Shannon children in his car and headed for the hospital. I ran across the dam again and up the hill to my parked car in which I drove to La Grange and turned in the alarm.

Here is Jerry Ormes's own account in *The Era*:

We rode to the upper end of the lake and turned around. As we headed back, the boat went across the wake and the bow started taking water.

Shannon gunned the motor to get the bow up, but this drove us into the wake and the boat was swamped. I grabbed my son and was hanging onto him when I saw my mother drowning. I went for her and lost my son.

Gene did all he could do. He did the best he could with the tools available. He was a hero.

A lot of the family died that day — six persons. *The Era* called it "One of the worst tragedies to ever to occur in Oldham County, and one of the worst boating accidents in the state." The dead included James Shannon, 36, owner of the boat; his wife, Thelma 27; two of their daughters, Carolyn 11 and Donna Sue 6; Mrs. Shannon's sister Mrs.

Juanita Ormes, 47; and Jerry Allen Ormes, the 14-month-old son of Mr. and Mrs. Jerry Ormes.

As a town we were shocked. As a town, we did what we have always done: we took care of our own and we buried our dead. I barely knew the victims but I was a pallbearer. Since there were too few family members left to be pallbearers, members of our football team were pallbearers and I was on the team.

I can remember clearly the day we buried the family members. It was at a cemetery that I had only seen from the road as we drove to St. Matthews: Louisville Memorial Gardens East. It was a spring day and the sun was shining as we put them in the ground. I helped carried the casket of one of the children.

I had always thought I was a sophomore or junior in high school when this happened. However, I was recently told that I was in the 8th grade at the time. That didn't seem right to me. But when I finally got a hard copy of *The Oldham Era* edition that had the story about the boating accident. I saw another story: "88 Will Graduate at La Grange School. "As I went down the list of "graduates" I saw my name among them — one of the few times my name had appeared in *The Oldham Era*. That story was directly next to the article about the boating accident.

My hometown. We took care of our own. Even though I did not know the victims who drowned, they were from LA. Thus, we, the town, mourned them and then buried them. We did not question it. We just did it.

I dwell on this aspect of LA simply because I have lived in numerous cities and life in those places has seemed to me very different than life in LA . Yes, the world is a village and while living in La Grange/Louisville I had a "village" of extended family and we all took care of each other. Certainly, Boston was not like that. When I would mention the "village" concept as being part of growing up in a small rural farm town in the South — I was met with a response I would later come to realize was a generalization of the South by Northerners. They thought Southerners were friendly to your face but the friendship was shallow. They felt New Englanders/New Yorkers/Chicago folks were more genuine in their friendship.

There is some truth to this, but not exactly what they seem to think. Usually in the cities you simply have a few close friends and that is "your family". But in LA everyone knew each other. Sure, there were some class distinctions but compared to what I have seen in the rest of America, they were nothing. We knew each other's parents. We knew each other's grandparents. We went to the same schools and had the same teachers. We all went to the same doctors. The same dentists. So, in our town, for the most part, there were no secrets. We knew each other from the day we were born. We celebrated together. We suffered together and we buried our dead together.

At least that is the LA of the Fifties and Sixties that I grew up in. And in many ways, there was no place better.

Chapter 4

OCCUPY Denver/Pushy Galore

It was a bad day at the Occupy demonstration. Raining hard and 38 degrees. When I woke up that morning and looked out my bedroom window, I knew that we would be seeing hypothermia patients. I have worked many a bicycle tour which started out warm and dry and then changed when a Colorado high-altitude summer rain and sleet storm hit. It got cold and wet going up the hills, but coming down from the top of an 11,000 to 12,000-foot pass the bicyclists started chilling to the point that it was hard to ride. Frozen hands, numb feet, soaked through and through, and sleet and ice all over the road. By the time they would get down from the pass they would be shivering uncontrollably. Especially bad were the "flat-landers" or people from the East or West Coast, who biked at sea level because, "It's July! How can I get hypothermia in July?" Easy. And they usually did not have enough layers.

The treatment for this is simple: a warming tent. Everyone goes into the tent. The folks shivering the worst are put close to the heaters. The people shivering with blue lips and hands and then they stop shivering — which is a very bad sign — they get to sit directly next to the heaters with wool blankets over their heads and shoulders. Same thing with slurred speech. A Patient that stops shivering and is slurring their speech is a Patient that is going into moderate to possibly severe hypothermia. Their treatment includes hot packs if you have them. We take their vitals every 5 minutes and ask them alert-and-oriented questions (A&O) before they're allowed to leave the tent. Anything under AxOx3 and they stay in the tent. Patients who were getting worse instead of better got serious treatment — a full workup and probably an ambulance ride.

The kids at the demonstration were walking around in wet clothes, shivering, and many had no hats. I immediately started barking orders to get in dry clothes and put on a hat. "Then take your wet clothes to a laundromat and get them dried!" I assured them that the political structure of the United States would not change by the time they got back with dry clothes.

When the lead medical volunteer showed up, I brought her up to date. "We have a pretty serious situation with hypothermia" I told her, adding that "we should set up a warming tent to dry people out." She replied, "Tents are illegal."

"I do not plan on being arrested," she added.

I was taken aback by what she said. In solidarity… No comment.

No warming tent.

She was handing out Vitamin C to everyone. She was obviously not a ski patroller. However, she was in charge, and this was my first day with the Occupy kids. I took a back seat.

The rain and cold continued and the marching did not really warm people up that much. So, after a couple of hours I left and went home, as did most of the protesters. I was not discouraged because I knew there would be other Occupy days. This was not my first rodeo.

At home I took a good long hot shower, ate some food, and took a nap. Waking up, coffee, then turned on my email to see what was going on. About 20 emails down was an email from someone calling themself — Pushy Galore.

Who on God's green earth is Pushy Galore? I wondered.

・ ・ ・

PUSHY GALORE

I read the email.

The woman whose email name was "Pushy Galore" turned out to be a person that I'd gone to high school with — a person I had not seen or heard from since 1969, over 40 years ago.

The name "Pushy Galore" was new. She was certainly not called "Pushy Galore" back when I knew her in high school. This email name she'd given herself was obviously a play on "Pussy Galore" from the James Bond movie "Goldfinger." But I could sort of see how it fit.

The woman I'd known 40 years ago was bright but very eccentric. Unfortunately for her, "eccentric" in a small rural high school in the South usually translates as "odd". I, and a lot of my classmates, found it very easy to make fun of Pushy simply because she was odd — or at least we considered her odd.

Back in high school, Pushy did not like me very much. I am sure that in her eyes I was an asshole. She actually asked in her email, "How did you make it out to Colorado?" Her tone was more like "How in the heck did you, of all people, make it to Colorado?" What she was not saying was that she considered me an idiot and never in her wildest dreams did she think I would amount to anything, much less be a success in Colorado. For those who do not know, Colorado is a place many Kentuckians strive to relocate to. Something about that "dry heat" in the summer. The Ohio River Valley can be pretty miserable in the summer. Colorado is a frequent vacation destination for Kentuckians and moving there permanently is a "step up." The equation being, folks from Kentucky really like to vacation in Colorado. However, I do not think I have ever met anyone in Colorado who dreams of going to Kentucky for a vacation. Nobody, that is, except me.

Anyway!

"Pushy Galore" as a name suddenly made sense to me. It was exactly the sort of name my classmate would give herself. The play and satire on sexism, and, for the record Pushy was pushy. That is, she was assertive, sort of. It all fit. Very creative. Perfect!

She always was smart.

Now, remembering her, and thinking about that name she'd given herself, I found myself flashing back to my puberty in a small Kentucky town when "Pussy Galore" was on the screen.

This saga took place in my hometown at a place called the Lakeview Drive In. The year was 1964 or thereabouts. I was growing up in a small farm town outside Louisville. Back then we Kentucky folks did not have many local national heroes other than basketball heroes. Hunter S. Thompson, a Kentucky boy, had not yet started writing for Rolling Stone and Tom Cruise and Johnny Depp (Kentucky claims them) were barely conceived, if conceived at all at that point. Muhammad Ali, or Cassius Clay as we knew him at that time, Louisville's Champ, was just beginning to win but was not famous yet.

Thus, we had little in American culture to be proud of. Then out of nowhere came a film called "Goldfinger." A sizzling hot James Bond film that was written up in Playboy Magazine (Playboy matters, or at least it matters to a 13-year-old boy), and part of it took place in Fort Knox, which is right outside Louisville!

A Hollywood film being shot in our part of the world. Not since the D. W. Griffith days had Louisville been in the Hollywood spotlight. We were psyched.

Although La Grange aka LA is now a suburb of Louisville, back when I was in puberty, LA was a long way from the movie theaters of Louisville. Most of us could not go to the movies unless our parents took us. "Goldfinger" was certainly not a movie that we wanted to see with our parents. We'd heard the rumors there was a hot naked woman painted in gold in the movie! We had all seen the photos in Playboy. When the film came to our local drive-in, The Lakeview, we were all waiting to see it.

The Lakeview Drive-In was a piece of art/folklore. We called it "the Pondview" because the "Lake" was actually a pond about one foot deep, choked with cattails and lily pads, that sustained a huge number of frogs. When I say "a huge number of frogs," I am not joking. These guys were croakers. You had to turn the volume all the way up on the drive-in's speaker just to drown out the frogs. Many of my high school classmates lost their virginity to the sound of those frogs barking out their war song.

Our film was coming! On Saturday night we rolled out in our various broken-down cars to watch the hot sex spectacle. I was not old enough to drive, so my ride was my sister and one of her friends. I was on a mission! My goal was to experience Pussy Galore to the maximum from the back seat of my sister's car.

Now the lure of Pussy Galore to a Southern male 13-year-old virgin should be obvious to our readers. Further, she was in Playboy, and considering what was going on around me in school and Southern society, this was definitely porn. Just the name was porn. How were people allowed to say things like "Pussy Galore"? Larry Flynt, another Kentuckian, had not yet started Hustler magazine. Free speech meant you could say "hell" at UK football games, as in "Give 'em hell, Cats!" Pussy Galore was not really in the mix.

The film was great. For once, the crowd actually kept it down pretty much and we watched the various Bond tricks take place. Although it was supposed to be located in Fort Knox, most of the action did not take place there and to be quite honest, who cared? I wanted to see what happened between Bond and Pussy Galore.

The film had been on for about an hour when suddenly the screen went blank.

Now this was not all that unusual. Film celluloid had broken before, reels of film had been lost, whatever. Delays were not unusual at the Pondview and we did not really think anything of it. The frogs continued their symphony during the delay and we waited and waited. After what seemed like forever to a Southern male 13-year-old wanting to see more Pussy Galore, an announcement came over the speakers: "In order to see the rest of the movie, you have to come back next Saturday night and we will show the rest of the movie."

For a brief moment, the frogs carried the air, but as soon as the information we had just heard started sinking into our brains, the car horns drowned out the frogs! It was outrageous!

We honked our horns for 10 or 15 minutes, but Pondview management would not budge.

The same announcement repeated. At some point the loudspeaker blared out, "Quit honking your horns and go home. Come back next Saturday to see the rest of the movie."" (The word "film" was not in their vocabulary.)

Finally, we went home. During the drive home we started laughing and we couldn't quit. Such a ridiculously hayseed, hillbilly event! Only in LA could a drive-in get away with such an absolutely wacko scheme to make money — and what made it especially hayseed is that everybody would come back next Saturday and pay again to see the rest of the movie.

Well, we did not go back next Saturday. In fact, it was years later before I finally saw the Ft. Knox scenes of "Goldfinger." Saturday Night at the Movies provided what the Pondview did not, but the Pondview was special.

A significant part of my teenage life was associated with that pond. I did not lose my virginity to the sound of the bullfrogs. Not because I was better than that, but simply because I was a bit of a nerd. I felt up and got felt up by my fair share of cowgirls at the Pondview, and to be quite honest about it, I would not trade those days for anything. I can remember many a summer night — or winter for that matter — driving out to the Pondview and watching a movie and all that went with it.

I am surprised that a film has not really captured that part of American society better. All those films and TV shows about the Fifties and drive-in eating facilities. I would have thought that they would have found a way to relive that memory of drive-in movie theaters. So far, the only director who's recreated that feeling is John Sayles, in his film "Lone Star," in which a scene at the drive-in is key to the story.

There was also a song called "Summer of '69," which was the year Pushy Galore and I graduated from high school. The song was sung by Bryan Adams (who was really about the age of 10 in 1969). It is an excellent song and the "drive in" part of that song was really good. However, other than that, the drive-in movie part of American folklore is simply gone. I am a little surprised that John Cougar Mellencamp has not included it in one of his songs. He does such an excellent job of capturing the Midwest/Southern rural experience in his music.

According to rumor, the frogs and the tradition of losing your virginity continued at the Pondview until one night when the concrete screen crumbled to the ground while a movie was playing. It has not been denied nor confirmed that the patrons of the movie that night got their money back.

About Pushy Galore: I wrote her back, and it turned out she was having some very serious problems at work. I told her I was a civil rights investigator and that I had handled many an employment case. I then apologized for my high school behavior and attempted to help her. The jury is still out on what happened to her and if she wants my help. I do owe it to her.

Pussy Galore/Pushy Galore! It is really just plain amazing how one e-mail 40 years later could bring the whole event/memory/treasure back in an instant.

When people have traumatic brain injuries (TBI) the docs attempt to find memories: film, music, old friends, anything, to help "bring them back." Well, Pushy Galore, you instantly brought me back to my youth, and it was a great youth. Oh yeah. Yes, I am very proud of my hayseed roots.

Thank you, Pushy Galore.

Chapter 5

Saying Good-bye to John

We went to kindergarten together and it is difficult to go back in life much further than kindergarten. Learning how to tie my shoes is probably the most important "skill" I learned in kindergarten. However, what I really learned in kindergarten was about people and life. Some of these first lessons about people have stayed with me ever since.

John was one of the strong ones. Some were not. I still have the photo of us all, somewhere. Too many from our kindergarten and 1st Grade are now gone: Ann, Donnie, Donald, and now John Shepherd have passed. Some moved away and I only remember their first names. Janet, her parents died suddenly and Janet moved away. We were all in school and then one day she was just gone and I never heard anything about her again. Another was Pam, a good childhood friend and now I have no idea where she went. Hopefully, she is still alive. Ann was always my contact on the kindergarten mates. She remembered better than I did and Ann passed away a few years ago.

I played Little League Football — or whatever it was called — in the 7th and 8th grades. In many ways Little

League Football was the social chemistry of LA. Fathers would come and watch their sons play and talk and lobby the coaches. Even as a pre-teen I could recognize the politics of this situation. I could see that fathers were lobbying to get their sons on the team or into playing a certain position. It was small-town pewee football politics. My dad was off doing doctor stuff and I do not think he attended one practice the entire time I played football in LA or at Oldham County High School.

Despite the politics of dads trying to jockey their boys onto the teams, sometimes an actual talent emerged. John was one. Although I used to hang with John a fair amount, I never learned who thought up the play that was to make John a starter on every football team on which he played. Maybe it was John's father but probably it was John that thought it up.

It was a great play: the ball was hiked, and almost immediately the quarterback would slightly jump into the air and toss the ball to John, who was directly in front of the quarterback. This play would almost always result in a gain of 3 or 4 yards. Sometimes much more. This was done at least once a game and maybe as much as three times in a game. It was a great first-down trick to catch them by surprise, or a third-down play when a few yards were needed for a first down. John scored more than a few touchdowns with this play.

You see, John was the right end and when the ball was hiked, John would immediately move laterally until he was directly in front of the quarterback. At that point the Q back would just toss the ball a few feet to John. One reason it worked so well was because John was tall and he had only to take a few steps in order to be in the perfect position.

We worked on this play in practice until it was down to a science. He was very fast at this move and in all our years of playing football I do not remember that John ever dropped the ball (an incomplete pass). The play was almost always a success. It was a play we would use in desperate times when we needed a first down very badly. So, John certainly earned his position as a starter. As I recall, he started every game from the time he was in the 7th grade until we went to high school, where John continued being a starter and continued using his secret play.

Life has a way of getting in the way of things sometimes. When I first started writing this, I thought

John played football his entire time at Oldham County High School. But then I looked through the yearbooks and discovered that the last time John was in the football photo was his freshman year.

I thought it happened his junior or senior year, but apparently John's father died late in his freshmen year or early in his sophomore year. After that, John was too busy with life to play football. His father was a great guy, like John, and everybody liked him. I know I liked him. John did not have any brothers, and when his Dad died, John became the man of the house. No small thing back in 1967 — especially for a sophomore in high school.

We graduated from Oldham County High in 1969.

We went to college.

Next time I hooked up with John was in the late Seventies. The Vietnam War came and went; we both graduated from college; he went to Optometry School in Chicago; I went to Boulder, Colorado for a while to be a hippie after graduating from U of L. I came back and we both ended up living in the Louisville area. I was working at a place called the Jefferson County Energy Conservation Office in the Jefferson County Courthouse. I started working for Todd Hollenback but eventually was working for Mitch McConnell in his first political office — County Judge of Jefferson County. John set up shop with his first wife in LA. Both were Optometrists.

LA is a small town and Dad and John became colleagues. Dad was about the only doctor in LA at that time, and he and John, an optometrist, became pals, and I re-hooked up with John as a friend. We both had similar political views, views that were pretty standard among young people who had attended college in larger cities during the Vietnam/Nixon/Watergate era. We were both pro-civil rights and anti-nuclear power/arms.

Public Service Indiana started building the Marble Hill Nuclear Power Plant in Madison, Indiana, less than 30 miles from LA. As I became more active in the fight against the Marble Hill plant, John and I got closer. Eventually, I along with John and Peggy Dillinger — started a group in LA called Oldham County for Safe Energy. John certainly helped out, a lot, but he preferred to keep a low profile since he was a local doctor and being a "no nukes" person was controversial (at least in the beginning it was controversial).

We did some really good work in LA educating folks about what nuclear power plants were and why they were dangerous. At one point, after the Three Mile Island disaster, the evacuation plans for Oldham County became a major stumbling block for Public Service Indiana. For those that do not know, every operating nuclear power plant has to have an evacuation plan so that all that live within 20 -25 miles of the plant can evacuate in minutes/hours if there is an accident. The evacuation plan was necessary in order to get the nuke licensed and operating. Until Three Mile Island happened, no one really paid attention to this sort of thing. However, after Three Mile Island, evacuation plans were a very necessary part of the licensing process. In other words, if there were no approved plans – the nuke could not receive its operating license.

Oldham County was within the designated distance of the evacuation area and several of our prominent politicians were hoping that Kentucky could stop the plant over the evacuation plans issue. The theory being that if Oldham County said it could not be evacuated in a few hours – then – technically — the plant could not go on line. At least that was the theory.

Suddenly, those meetings of the Oldham County Commissioners became very important to a lot of people and John and I were selected to go to the Oldham Country Commissioners regarding the issue. It was the same thing in Trimble County. We were moderately successful. However, the evacuation disputes were never cleared up because Marble Hill never went on line (operational).

The plant was closed down because Public Service Indiana simply ran out of money to build the thing. After Three Mile Island, Wall Street Banks quit investing in nuclear power because it was viewed as a bad investment. Public Service Indiana simply ran out of money to build the thing and the evacuation issue was never resolved. Lack of money and Wall Street Banks pulling out of the nuclear power business started happening all over the country – not just at Marble Hill. The end result being nationwide, was that evacuation plans became a non-issue because the nuclear power industry collapsed.

Or – a better way to say it is – we won!

It was a real comfort knowing John in those years. The tear gas of busing in Louisville was still settling and the war in Vietnam was still fresh in everyone's mind. The President of the United States (Nixon) had resigned just a few years earlier due to misconduct. Having someone in my hometown with similar views on any level was a relief. We bonded.

Many of the anti-nuclear activists in Louisville got to know John and he became their optometrist. He was a very good eye doctor. Even after I moved to Boston, with all its medical facilities, I would come home during the holidays and let John check my eyes. Partly, because he would do it for free but mostly because he was a damn good eye doctor.

We stayed friends. We went to our 20th high school reunion at Dykes Restaurant in 1989. I flew home for the event. He had remarried by then and I remember telling John that he had to go to the reunion or I wouldn't go. We both went and we both had a good time at the reunion. I have always had a great time with Class of '69 folks and Oldham County High School folks in general. High school was one of the best times in my life and I really enjoyed my friendships there.

After the reunion, I flew back to Boston and became involved with the woman who would become my life partner. We lived in Boston for a few years then moved to Colorado in 1990. I had not been home to La Grange for some time, but I came back when Dad died in 1992. I saw

John at Dad's funeral. He was very shaken up at my dad's death — it surprised me to see how much my father's death affected him. I had known for about a year that Dad had leukemia, so I guess I had been preparing myself, but when I saw John at the funeral home he was visibly shaken.

Dad's funeral was the last time I saw John. I was a little surprised when John did not attend the 40th Class of 69 reunion in 2009.

After Dad died, my trips home to LA decreased significantly. I had a new life in Colorado and did not start making trips back to LA until I retired in 2008. Then I started coming back to LA on a regular basis and frequently, I would ask Beverly, my Dad's second wife, or my anti-nuclear activist friends in Louisville about John and nobody seemed to know where he was or what he was doing. They said they'd been looking for him too because he was such a good eye doctor.

And then, one day while doing training laps around Cherokee Park on my bicycle, I got a call from Beverly and she said that John had died. I did not even know he was sick.

And just like that — John is gone. He was a great guy and I miss him still. I sincerely wish I'd seen him one last time to let him know what a good guy and good friend he had been.

Words cannot express my feelings.

Rest in peace, John.

Chapter 6

Westport

Every trip home I always go to Westport. Usually I go to La Grange as well, but sometimes I just make the trip down US 42 past Goshen and turn into the road going to Westport and skip going to LA. There are several reasons for this. First, the "hill" going down to Westport from U.S. 42 is an excellent hill to train on for bicycling. Living in Colorado, I am used to climbing mountains on my bike but usually these 5 miles+ climbs are not as steep as the hill out of Westport. So, when I am in Kentucky to be a medic on bike rides, I will go out to Westport and ride. Good training.

The second reason I go to Westport is that some of my best memories in life were formed in Westport.

Growing up I barely knew the place existed. I remember my mom dragged my sister and me over to Westport to "discover" some graves. My mom was a history nut and was always trying to find a graveyard where confederate soldiers, slaves, or just plain famous people were buried. Those days! Too young to revolt, I had to obey. She would take us and our box of cornmeal to these gravestones. The reason we had cornmeal was to rub it on a gravestone so that we could read the writing — the name, date of birth, date of death, and other details, like "CSA" on the stone, which stands for "Confederate States of America." We did this at gravesites all over Oldham County; a few times we went to Westport. By the way, the cornmeal thing works.

There were also some sort of Indian burial grounds or Indian burial mounds outside Westport but we never really did much with that. And when the river flooded, the whole family would drive over to Westport to see how high the water was.

Then I went to high school. Girls and beer! Field parties gave way to just going over to Westport and partying on the river. Too many times I did this. I am absolutely sure the "state boys" — the Kentucky State Police, that is — knew we'd be over there. But in my high school days there were different partying factions and usually my group was considered beginners, or "nothing to worry about". We did not get into fights, and except for experimenting with sex and drinking until we got sick, we were pretty harmless. So only one in every five parties or so did the cops come break things up. Most of the time they just left us alone. Almost never did anyone get arrested – at least I never got arrested.

Those parties over on the Ohio River at Westport were very much part of my growing up in America. Although it was the latter 1960s, La Grange and Oldham County seemed far from the struggle America was going through. We were just dumb kids growing up.

Usually it would go something like this: Get in the car and pick up the gang, and drive to Westport. Gasoline was around 25 cents a gallon back then and putting on a hundred miles or so a night was not a big deal. If we knew we were going to Westport we would drive to Prospect, to the liquor store on the Jefferson County/Oldham County line, and find someone to buy us some beer. We were all underage, so usually some sort of bribe was involved: We'd pay for a pint of vodka or whisky or whatever booze the guy buying us the beer wanted; that was the payment. A couple of times we were just ripped off doing this. The guy just took off with our money without getting us our beer, but usually this went off without a hitch.

Once we got the beer, it was over to Westport.

I probably partied at Westport more in 1968 and 1969 than at any other time. These were my Junior and Senior years. On many occasions my pals and I would "park" at Westport with our dates on hot summer nights. The humidity was thick over by the river and the urge would hit to go skinny-dipping, which we did. To my knowledge none of us got any sort of infections from the water, which is a wonder. Even now I am told by my ER medical pals that to go into the Ohio is asking for an infection from god-knows-what. Fifty years ago, the river was not a pretty site in terms of toxins and contaminants, and the risk of infections was considerably higher. However, being dumbass kids and unbreakable at that age, we all survived it.

These good times came at a price. I distinctly remember my mother arranging an "intervention" regarding my partying and drinking. Even my Dad attended. He actually lowered his newspaper and came to the family gathering place, the kitchen table, as Mom started the drilling. After doing a very bad job of negotiating for myself, I eventually said simply that every time the Belle of Louisville went by on the river, we would have a beer. Of course, that was utter bullshit. Actually, it was not total bullshit — we did drink a beer every time the Belle went by, especially Derby weekend. However, we also "killed a lot of soldiers" when the Belle was not going by. As was typical, my Dad did not say a word the entire time. He looked pretty bored by the whole thing. I am sure he would have rather been reading his paper, which is exactly what he did as soon as my mother let him leave the room.

I survived the intervention and returned to being a party animal my entire Senior year.

Most of my memories are good ones, of fun and camaraderie, experiments with sex, and so on; taking off our clothes and wading into the river. I never cut my foot on glass, which is also a wonder, because we certainly threw a huge number of bottles into the river. Every time a barge or The Belle went by, we would throw bottles at them, as hard as we could.

About the swimming: Usually we could wade out a good 30 to 60 feet in water only knee-to hip-deep, but then it got much deeper very fast. So really, we were just wading, not swimming. Although I was a very good swimmer in those days, I never took the challenge to swim across to Indiana and back. I am pretty sure I could have done it. As a high school kid, I was very disappointed that OCHS did not have a swim team. (Nor did they have a bicycle team or a ski team, which I would have liked very much.)

I probably could have made the swim over to Indiana and back; but in my head I'd always hear a nagging lectures–– even after too many beers — about the middle of the river having some serious currents that were not to be messed with. I'd already had enough "events" in water to know that bad things could happen. Once I got swept away by currents in a Smokey Mountain rain-choked river, and if not for my dad's quick actions I would have been gone. Same thing with the undertow in Florida when I was in early grade school. The undertow took me out past the breakers and I could not get back. I swam sideways (as I was repeatedly told to do) and made it back to shore, but I knew the fear that comes when you suddenly realize that the water is in control and you are not.

Our way of beating the heat and the angst of being young was to go over to Westport and let loose. Sometimes we built fires, cooked food, and drank lots of beer. I believe that more of my classmates lost their virginity at the Pondview Drive-In (that is, the Lakewood Drive In) than at Westport, but it was a toss-up. It would certainly be interesting to find out the answer to that question. Perhaps a questionnaire at the 50th Class Reunion.

Although for the most part it was just plain good clean teenage American fun, there were some serious moments. I remember finding out that one of my classmates had been driving back to Westport after making a beer run and did not make the curve at the bottom of the Westport hill. He flipped his Ford Falcon and ended up in an ambulance. I did not find out if he went to the ER. Hopefully not. My dad probably would have been the one fixing him up and Dad never said anything.

Probably one of the best ways to describe our times in Westport is a song by Garth Brooks. "Ain't going down till the sun comes up" pretty much summarizes my life in those days. It was before Woodstock. Before Kent State and before Nixon resigned. It was during a time when the body bag count from Vietnam was significantly on the increase; Martin Luther King and Bobbly Kennedy were assassinated. The same times as the Democratic Convention in Chicago and the hippies moving into Haight-Ashbury. The Grateful Dead were just starting out; Jefferson Airplane put out a song called "Revolution";

Timothy Leary was preaching, telling us to take acid; and for the first time I saw a white man kiss a black woman on television. In a Star Trek show Captain Kirk kissed Lt. Uhura – a passionate kiss!

It was also a time when Title VIII of the Civil Rights Act of 1968 was passed, and a time when Public Service of Indiana was thinking seriously about building a nuclear power plant in Madison, Indiana.

We in Oldham County watched Walter Cronkite report the events on our televisions after dinner and before we did our homework, and, to be honest about it, I had no idea what was really going on in America. What I did know is that I was now eligible for the draft. Summer came and we headed to Westport.

About the town of Westport: There is a scene in the film "How The West Was Won" when the family is floating down river — the Ohio — on their raft and they pull in for the night to buy some goods, but it turns out the store is run by river pirates, and there's a fight to the death. It being Hollywood, the good guys win. I always thought that in real life this event would have taken place in Westport. I was only 12 when I saw the movie and it kind of fit what I had heard about Westport. Once, it was a flourishing, booming, river town that had gotten its start back during the days of the Revolutionary War. I checked on the history and learned that Westport had a Post Office in 1815. Also, being 12 years old, I fell in love with Debbie Reynolds, the star of that movie.

About the river pirates: back when I used to party in Westport, there was a shack with a sign that said "River Pirates of the Ohio" or something like that. Which brings me to another film called "Striking Distance" starring Bruce Willis. It takes place in Pittsburgh and the Ohio River plays a major role in the movie. In the movie when Bruce is a kid growing up along the Ohio River, he runs with a group of kids who had a shack called the "Ohio River Pirates." Close enough names that when I saw the film I immediately thought of Westport. In the movie, Bruce lives on a houseboat on the Ohio, which is something I have always wanted to do. And he has a girlfriend, Sarah Jessica Parker. A lot of the girls I took to Westport looked as good as her. Especially when they were Juniors at OCHS.

Anyway.

"Striking Distance" is a cop thriller. A high point comes when Bruce stops to let Jessica off his boat onto one of the pilings of a bridge — or is it the other way around? I always wanted to do that and I guess if I start kayaking the Ohio, I may do it. I used to sea kayak off the coast of New England. The one thing I quickly learned then is that the North Atlantic will swallow you up and not even leave a trace of your existence. In a heartbeat. One moment you and everything you love is there, and then — in a moment — it is all gone.

Somehow, I feel like the Ohio River will have a little bit more mercy and grace than the North Atlantic. So, one of these days when I go home to visit, I need to rent a kayak and venture out to the bridge's pilings just to check things out.

As a flourishing river town, Westport had its fair share of river mansions and all that goes with it. Westport was developed before La Grange was even a speck on the map, back in the days when the river was everything. A time before railroads, cars, interstates, or airplanes. Westport had its moment with riverboats and dance hall girls. Everything Mark Twain says about the Mississippi was true at Westport, our town on the "Banks of the Ohio."

I have crossed the Mississippi several times at St. Louis and am always amazed at how small the Mississippi River is there compared to the Ohio at Louisville. The Mississippi should have been called the Ohio River all the way from Pittsburgh to New Orleans. It is a mighty river in the heart of America and it should have been called the Ohio. All the way to the delta!

Now I sometimes think about moving to Westport, but the real estate is a little too expensive and the town is a little too far from Louisville or even La Grange. It is certainly within my grasp and there is an appeal for me, as a bicyclist, writer, and also as someone that always wanted to play on the Ohio River. However, part of being an adult, which I call myself now, is realizing that memories are good, but they are not life.

So, every time I go back to Louisville I go back to Westport and relive a few memories and a time when life was much simpler and I loved so many people and they loved me back. I had a great youth and Westport and the Ohio River are part of it.

Chapter 7

Tornadoes

I had just eaten lunch and was walking back from the Student Center back to the photo lab at the University of Louisville. I needed a lunch break because I had just developed six rolls of film, which is tedious and tiring. This was prior to digital cameras, and developing film required going into a darkroom with absolutely no light, no dust, and no moving air. Any light at all would destroy the film, and dust was a photographer's nightmare. Dust getting on your negative while it was developing would cause a dark spot or a white spot right in the middle of the negative — permanent damage to your negative. Such were the days of celluloid.

Probably the worst case of developing-film failure ever was on D Day, one of the most important days in the twentieth century. Robert Capa, a famous war photojournalist, landed on Omaha Beach with the first wave of American soldiers. He shot several rolls of film of the utter confusion and horror of the landings. Then he gave his film to the "darkroom technician" to develop. The technician botched the job and destroyed all but 10 shots of some of the most important photography of the twentieth century. The 10 pics that survived were the basis for much of the visual effects in "Saving Private Ryan." At least that is what I have read.

Developing film is not fun. It is a delicate task, hard to do. I had just developed six rolls of film and had not eaten since breakfast. It was early afternoon so I took a lunch break and went to the Student Center cafeteria for a burger. My usual. The food hit the spot and now I was walking back to the photo lab.

It was April in Kentucky and the April-showers-brings-May-flowers thing was not happening. Major storms had been coming through the Ohio River Valley for days now and today was no different. It did not look that bad when I started walking to the Student Center — it was only about 100 yards — but now, walking back, the weather was bizarre. The sky was bright and blue in part of the sky, very dark in other parts. As I looked East, a light shade of green. Raining in one area and bright sun in another. It looked like snow or sleet was falling a hundred yards away. Odd. But the wind was not even blowing. It was not stable weather.

And as I was walking, the sirens went off. This was not all that unusual in Kentucky. Tornado sirens were going off all the time in the Spring. I lit a cigarette and kept walking.

And then it happened: A finger of a tornado came down out of the cloud and clipped the silos over at the Purina plant a couple hundred yards away. It happened fast, and debris was flying — but it was not coming my way.

And of course, I just stood there.

I had my camera with me and probably this was the photo shot of my life. I was in my second year as a photography major and this could have been the beginning of my career — for sure a cover photo in *The Courier-Journal* newspaper, and my career as a photojournalist would be taking off. Yes, even the possibility that it would make the cover of Look, Time, or Life magazine.

What I had just witnessed was probably the most important potential photograph of my career. Yes, I recognized the importance of what I was seeing, and yes, I would have dropped everything and taken my career-making photograph — but I had no film in my camera. I had just developed all the rolls of film I had.

I had my camera with me because you always take your camera with you so that it would not be stolen. A $250 camera was a lot of money in 1974. If there had been film in my camera it is quite possible that my entire life would have been different from that moment forward.

I walked back to the photo lab and told them I had just seen a tornado hit the Purina silos. As the assistant to the photography professor, I had a little authority, but the general reaction of my fellow darkroom comrades was something like, "Yeah, sure you did." "What is Scott smoking?" However, the ribbing was over soon enough. We always had a radio on in the darkroom to keep us from going crazy from the boredom, and soon the programming was interrupted. The whole east end of Louisville was being destroyed by tornadoes. Sirens all over the city were going off and everyone was being advised to seek shelter, which we did not do. We all started trying to get home. I closed the photo lab and did just like everybody else, I headed home.

I was living at my parents' house in La Grange about 30 miles from Louisville. I tried to call them but all the phones lines were down (Yes — there was a time before cell phones). I knew they would be worried about me.

Actually, I was worried about them. Just a few days before, on April 1, a tornado had touched down in Campbellsburg, only a few miles from my parents' house. Folks heard the sirens and went down into their basements and then came out after the storm had passed and for all practical purposes, the town was gone. The downtown was destroyed, at least that is what the news said.

Now it seemed that this tornado, from what we were hearing on the radio, was much worse than the one that destroyed Campbellsburg. So, I started the drive home. The shortest route was on I-65, the north-south expressway, and from there to I-71.

The damage on I-65 was not that bad, but on I-71, east of the Watterson, the highway was littered with everything from refrigerators to house tops. I had to drive around one house roof which was sitting on the road in the eastbound lane. The eastern suburbs along U.S.42 had been clobbered. Everything imaginable in a house was now on I-71. No bodies, I am glad to say, and I did not see any dead cats or dogs either — but I saw lawnmowers, TVs, cars — yes, cars! Bed mattresses, refrigerators. Lots of refrigerators, table saws, couches, washers, dryers, lamps, books, golf cubs – anything and everything people have in their house was on I-71.

It was a very slow drive home but I did get there. and to be honest about it, I do not think my parents and I had ever been so happy to see each other.

Our house had been spared! Completely! No damage. A few trees were down, but nothing unusual about that. Nearly all communications were out. Our phone, the TV. The only thing working was the radio. Shortly after I arrived home the State Police showed up and took my dad, the town doctor, to the hospital because patients were pouring in and our phones were not working. No lights.

It was a very long night.

The next morning, I drove through La Grange and except for some downed trees and telephone poles, it did not seem that bad. I did not see any houses that had been destroyed. Absolutely nothing like driving along I-71 and seeing hundreds of houses seriously damaged, with their roofs gone. Downtown LA had survived.

I believe the La Grange Courthouse lawn lost a few of its great trees. Probably pin oaks, because they are so huge and tall; they do not bend and they have relatively small root systems. When a force like the tornados that hit Louisville comes along, they are just blown over. Usually pin oaks did not break; they were just uprooted.

Cherokee Park in Louisville lost hundreds of pin oaks. Along Bardstown Road and Eastern Parkway, the downed pin oaks took out phone and electrical wires. Bardstown Road looked like a war zone, as did much of the city. Crescent Hill was hit hard. Hundreds of giant trees fell on cars and houses, taking power and phone lines with them.

Over 900 homes were destroyed in the Louisville area. The good news is there were only 3 deaths. Considering the magnitude of the tornadoes, Louisville got off lucky.

There were no deaths in La Grange, but in Brandenburg, Ky., about 35 miles as the crow flies west from Louisville, 31 were killed and many more were injured. The tornado that hit Brandenburg was an F5, the only F5 tornado in Kentucky history. The town was changed forever. So much damage and so many deaths. The locals started describing events as, "Before the tornado" or "After the tornado." It was a defining moment in their lives, the same way that Americans now describe events pre or post 9/11.

This monster tornado system — the "1974 Super Outbreak" — reached from Alabama to Canada. A total of 71 people were killed in Kentucky. Eleven were killed in Madison and Hanover, Indiana and 90 percent of Hanover was destroyed.

I had a girlfriend back then, my college sweetheart, and she lived in Newark, Ohio, so I knew a lot of the towns between Cincinnati and Columbus on I-71. The tornado literally followed I-71 up the state, destroying town after town along the way. Washington Court House, Xenia, and all the way up to Canada.

Kentucky had the second largest number of fatalities with 71 and Alabama had the highest with 77. Indiana had 47 Ohio had 38 and Tennessee had 45. The list goes on.

• • •

All this happened over 40 years ago but it is funny, "unusual" is a better word, unusual when the memories of such events will surface. A good 20 years after the tornadoes I was working in Denver at a federal agency and my supervisor mentioned that he had lived in Ohio at one point. I mentioned the tornadoes and he remembered — vividly — the day the tornado hit Washington Court

House in Ohio. As we both sat there — a pause in the daily routine of "running America" as we did in federal agencies — America was put on hold. Both of us were stopped dead in our tracks as we remembered that day in April. For us it was like remembering the day that Kennedy was shot or the day we heard about Kent State, he being from Ohio and I being from Kentucky. Although many other disasters have happened in America, this one was major and it seems that except for the folks who had been directly affected by it, many did not remember it. We were the only ones in our office who seemed to know about these tornadoes. The moment we discussed the tornados a small bond was instantly formed.

It was not until decades later that I learned how important those tornados that destroyed the Ohio River Valley and rampaged through the South and the Midwest were to all of us. Now that I am retired, frequently I will write or work at home with The Weather Channel on as background noise. I pick The Weather Channel because weather is key to everything I do in retirement — cross-county skiing, alpine skiing, hiking, bicycle rides. So, I watch The Weather Channel.

Part of what I do requires driving across Kansas and eastern Colorado on my way back to Kentucky. Kansas and eastern Colorado are "tornado country." On more than one occasion I have had to plan my trip back East around The Weather Channel's forecast. I have been caught by tornados in Kansas and it is not fun but that is another story. I closely monitor the Weather Channel, so that I am not caught by a twister in Kansas or on the plains of eastern Colorado.

One day while watching the "Tornado Forecast" it was mentioned that the tornado forecasting system was a by-product of the April 1974 Tornado Outbreak. After that string of tornadoes and the huge death toll — as well as the millions of dollars in damage that occurred — something had to be done to protect people and property. I learned that this was when the current tornado warning system was developed. And it works — or at least it works as well as a warning system can work. Nothing can stop tornadoes.

In 2011 there was another Super Outbreak of tornadoes which ripped through the South and killed 346 people and did over $11 million in damages. Over 300 tornadoes were involved. One can only imagine how many more would have died if the Tornado Warning System had not been put in place as a result of the 1974 Outbreak.

On a personal level, it is funny — "odd" is a better word — it is odd that the next major natural disaster in the U. S. after the tornadoes of 1974 was the Big Thompson Flood in Ft. Collins, Colorado in 1976. One hundred forty-five people were killed. As life would have it, after graduating from the University of Louisville I moved to Boulder, Colorado right after that flood. The year was 1976, the year Colorado was picked to host the Winter Olympics and the Governor of Colorado informed the Olympic Committee that Colorado did not want the Olympics (I believe that was probably the only time that ever happened).

It was also the same year Claudine Longet killed her boyfriend Olympic Skier, Spider Sabich in Aspen. Apparently, Spider was running around on her and she wanted to stop it. And she did — she stopped him from living. I believe the defense was, "I did not know the gun was loaded." She was found guilty of negligent homicide and did 30 days in jail. Claudine's husband Andy Williams was friends with all the Kennedys. I am not sure which is more important, being friends with the Kennedys or killing someone in Aspen (Yes, Hunter Thompson was in

Aspen then.). The quick answer is, "she got off lucky." But that is a different story that I will write about someday.

About my career as a photojournalist: I continued with photography for years after the "tornado pic" did not happen. I even stooped so low as to be a part of a Photo Kid Workshop in Denver when I lived in Boulder. I say this as an "artist" totally condescending toward that type of photography. Actually, I worked in the negative room, filing the thousands of negatives, and was working my way up to being a kid photographer. As superior as I felt, the photographers taking photos of kids were making between $10 and $20 per hour and drove new cars. I was making $2.50 per hour and drove a complete wreck that barely made it to Colorado. And I was thankful for the $2.50 per hour. In other words, I would have sold out in minutes if I had been given the chance.

There were people who did take tornado pics that April day in 1974, and their photos did get in *The Courier-Journal*. Not on the front page, but on the cover of *The Courier-Journal Sunday Magazine* — which had even more prestige.

My Environment professor at Speed Scientific, Dr. Hugh Spencer, was taking a field trip with his class down to Muhlenberg County. Yes, the same Muhlenberg County that John Prine wrote about. The same Muhlenberg County John Denver made famous throughout the world when he sang the song Paradise (Muhlenberg County). When in Switzerland, rather than resorting to describing where I came from by mentioning Kentucky Fried Chicken, which they have in Switzerland, I took the high road and started singing the song "Paradise." Typically, about that time, someone would ask, in broken English, "is there really a Muhlenberg County?"

Anyway, I was a student of Dr. Spencer's and his trips to Muhlenberg Country were an annual event. When I was his student, we took the same trip to Muhlenberg County since as the song describes, Muhlenberg County is visibly an environmental disaster on a gigantic scale.

As Dr. Spencer and his class were taking their field trip, they were going down the Interstate when Doc Spencer looked up and saw a perfectly formed twister, probably about an F2, directly in front of him, no more than a mile away. He stopped the car and took the photo, and it appeared on the front page of *The Courier-Journal Magazine*. It was a perfect photo. In focus; the correct F stop; and framed correctly. Still, I believe a tornado hitting the Purina Silos – with debris flying in all directions would have "beaten" Doc Spencer's photo for the cover shot. A case of "Almost famous."

As for my photography career, it is true that if I'd had film in my camera that fateful day it is quite possible that my entire life would have been different. Photography is one of those arts that once you are "noticed" then the rest is up to you to hustle. Probably if I'd had film in my camera I would have been noticed.

After I graduated from U of L I went to live in Boulder, Colorado for a while. Boulder locals were always protesting and getting arrested out at Rocky Flats, which was literally just a few miles from where I was living. At that time, it was impossible to live in Boulder and not be educated about the production of plutonium triggers necessary for nuclear weapons, which were being made at Rocky Flats in Boulder. There were constant demonstrations to the point that even I noticed.

When I returned to Louisville, the same Dr. Hugh Spencer who took the tornado photo told me about a nuclear power plant they were building locally, close to Louisville. It was the Marble Hill Nuclear Power Plant in Madison, Indiana and as the crow flies it was not far from my parents' house in LA. I learned that all nuclear power plants are first-strike targets in a war. He also told me about a group that was organizing against the plant. I checked them out and found out about a demonstration they were having in New Albany and attended the demo.

I took a lot of photos that day, but never developed the film. I became involved in the fight to stop Marble Hill and I put down my camera and never picked it up again. And my life truly did change at that moment. Forever.

Chapter 8

Danny

My father died in 1992. If there is anything to be considered good news in losing one of, if not the most important person in my life, it is that we had about a year between when he was diagnosed with Leukemia and when he passed.

I made a lot of trips home to Kentucky to see him.

On one of those trips Dad was talking to his wife as we were getting ready to drive in to Louisville to have dinner, and in passing he mentioned that Danny Shearer was living with some friends over on the river. I was a little surprised because I had not heard of Danny in decades.

Danny had been a star in Oldham County when I was growing up. Everyone in the county knew his name. He was famous to us and the fact that I had not heard of him in years was a surprise.

I had been away from La Grange for over two decades and I still thought the clothing store Jones and Shearer's was open on Main Street and for all I know, it still was. I wanted to hear more about Danny, but I was home visiting my Dad, possibly for the last time. So, I did not inquire further. I simply noted it.

The next time I heard about Danny was over two decades after Dad died. An old friend from Oldham County put a photo of Danny's gravesite on Facebook. I printed it out and put it on my refrigerator. I would look at the photo of his gravestone and think, "I should write about Danny."

The Facebook post noted that Danny was "Mr. Basketball" and the person sending the photo also mentioned that Danny was "Mr. Basketball." I remembered instantly, I was there, in person, the day Danny Shearer became "Mr. Basketball" in Oldham County. I remember it like it was yesterday, even though I was only 12 years old.

America was a different country then. When Danny became "Mr. Basketball", the President of the United States of America was John F. Kennedy. Almost all of what we now call "The Sixties" had not happened. It was a different world. However, one thing was not different. Every March Kentuckians anxiously await the "Sweet 16" High School Basketball Tournament. In 1963 the tournament was in Freedom Hall, in Louisville. It was at that tournament in 1963 that Danny Shearer became "Mr. Basketball" and I was there.

Winters are cold in Kentucky. I now live in Colorado, and before that I lived in Boston, and in both places, they think of Kentucky as being in the South. To them, that means warm weather during winter or at least warmer than Denver or Boston. They are wrong.

I can remember winters where the lake behind my parents' house froze. I am talking about a big lake, not a pond. Crystal Lake is about a mile long and at least a hundred yards wide. A big lake. Many winters the lake would freeze 3 to 5 inches deep with ice and we would be able to skate on the lake for weeks. The Ohio River would freeze sometimes, too, and people would walk across the river on the ice.

My point in this is to remind folks that a 12-year-old boy in La Grange, Kentucky had nothing to do after he did his homework on winter nights. And by "winter night" I am talking about winter nights that started by the time you got home from school at 4 or 5. After dinner it was dark and very cold outside. I lived in the country and being a 12-year-old obviously I could not drive. So, unless we were going ice skating, what I did for entertainment was listen to basketball games on WHAS radio. Usually it was the University of Kentucky or the University of Louisville playing at Freedom Hall or on the road, but sometimes it was a high school game. I would sit by the radio for hours keeping stats: number of free throws; number of rebounds; number of points per player; on and on. I suspect this was my parents' plan to keep me from watching TV, and it worked. Like many Kentuckians, I was becoming a basketball nut!

The best games were the high school games I could attend in person. If I was lucky my mom or a friend's mom or dad was attending the OCHS Colonels game that night and I would tag along. Especially nice was when there were tournaments and there would be game after game, night after night. I got my clipboard and started keeping records of rebounds, shots hit, shots missed, number of fouls, point totals for each player. Like most people in Kentucky, I was no longer becoming a basketball nut. I was a basketball nut!

The Oldham County gym was a great place for ball games, and the stands would be filled. I guess I was not the only one that was bored to death on those nights that started at 5pm and were colder than a dog. It was a great show! The pep band was good and OCHS had very attractive cheerleaders (especially to a 12-year-old male). All my friends would be there. It was the Best Show in Town and the Oldham County Colonels were usually pretty good, which helped.

In 1963 the Oldham County Colonels were very good. As in maybe–going-to-State good!

I do not specifically remember the playoff games in 1963. I am not sure if they were played in Oldham County or at the Henry County Gym. I am also not sure whether in 1963 the Henry County Gym had been built. Now, the Henry County Gym is almost obsolete, but in the 60s the Henry County Gym was brand new and it was huge. It was a fantastic place for a ball game and it was not all that far away. I went to a lot of games there. We had many of the regional playoffs there simply because it was such a great gym. It could seat up to five thousand fans. It was the biggest and nicest gym in the region. However, I am not sure if it was built in time for the 1963 playoffs.

Most of my memories of the '63 Colonels were the times they were playing in our gym. Names like Ronnie Webster, Bobby Jenkins, Billy Mathis, Todd Roberts, and Danny Shearer. There were no bench warmers; everybody played a lot. The rest of the team was Pete Wright, Eddie Wilhoyte, Billy Brown, Gary Chisholm, Jackie Swann, David Prather, and Keith Oglesby. Now it is a little hard, but when I was 12 I knew all these players on sight, and my friends and I became so infatuated with them that we talked about them like they were our personal friends: "Eddie is moving kind of slow tonight — do you think maybe something is wrong?" "Danny has the eye tonight — three swooshes tonight!" (A "swoosh" was a shot from a long distance by a player. When the ball went into the basket, it didn't even touch the rim and just the net, making a "swoosh" sound and 2 points.) This is 1963, before the 3-point rule.

We talked about them as though we sat around and watched TV with them at night and went to school with them during the day. Not true, but we admired them so much we put them on a first-name basis. So did the whole county. At the barber shop where I went for my haircuts everyone talked about Todd or Ronnie like they'd had Sunday dinner with them every week of their lives. The 1963 Colonels basketball team were our heroes.

I actually was on a first-name basis with Todd Roberts and Danny. Todd lived on 4th Street and I'd grown up on

5th Street, one block over. Danny could always be found hanging around his mother's store, Jones and Shearer's, which my mother visited just about every time she went to town. I always felt cool when either of the guys said, "Hi Scott" if they saw me.

Another great thing about going to the games were the cheerleaders. I was a 12-year-old boy and they were 16 to 18-year-old young women. It being America in the early 60s, members of the cheerleader squad were selected for their attractive appearance and popularity in addition to their athletic ability. They were very attractive and very physically mature. I will let the reader fill in the blanks as to why a 12-year-old boy would like the cheerleader squad. My 12-year-old male friends and I had some extremely creative conversations about the cheerleaders. We were all really just starting into puberty, the hiding-Playboy-magazine-in-your-closet stage of puberty. Most of those cheerleaders, we thought, could have been in Playboy if they'd wanted to be. And most of them were dating members of the OCHS basketball team. We 12-year-old boys endlessly discussed the possibilities that presented themselves with OCHS Cheerleaders and OCHS Basketball players dating.

The cheerleaders were very good at what they did. They constantly had us on our feet making noise for the boys — cheering them on. Many were the times I came home from the basketball game with my voice hoarse from "cheering" so much.

The games were addictive. I went to as many of them as I could. In 1963 we were winning all the time, which, of course made for an even a better time. Naturally, this sort of good time spreads in a small county like Oldham, and the fact that we kept winning — more than anyone could remember ever winning in the past — made going to the basketball games sort of a movement. And it was growing.

Finally, it was time for the playoffs. OCHS won our division — the 8th Division. We were "going to State" — the "Sweet 16" Kentucky High School Basketball Tournament in Louisville, at Freedom Hall at the Fairgrounds!

I-71 had not been built in 1963. There were several standard routes people in Oldham County would take to get to Freedom Hall. Folks living over by the river would take the US 42 into Brownsboro, and then get on the Watterson Expressway, getting off at the Kentucky State Fairground exit to Freedom Hall. Back in those days US

42 was a very busy road, a two-lane blacktop — the main road between Louisville and Cincinnati. There was a lot of semi-trailer truck traffic on it, and it was very dangerous. Traveling down to Louisville to attend the basketball tournament was no small potatoes.

Folks in La Grange, Ballardsville, or Smithfield would drive to the high school in Buckner, then take Hwy. 22 to Crestwood and Pewee Valley and meet up with fans there, then drive through Anchorage to Middletown to get onto the Watterson there.

Hundreds of us went to the playoff games at Freedom Hall.

My mother took my sister Pat, me, and our friends to the games. We'd take as many kids as the car would hold. Everyone wanted to go to the games. As I remember, the games seemed to be going on round the clock, so sometimes we would have to get an early start, but it was worth it.

We won the first game of the series against Hancock County. Bobby Jenkins scored 33 points. OCHS fans went wild! The number of folks driving to the games became even bigger. Hundreds of us now became over a thousand of us, and the Colonels' cheering section became huge. It was like an epidemic had hit the county. Before the tournament we were winning and now we were in the tournament, and we were still winning. The cheerleaders kept us on our feet for entire games and the thought that we could win State went from being a whisper to normal chit chat. Like we had always expected to win state.

The press started calling the Oldham County Colonels "The Cinderella Team."

Our next game was with Newport Catholic and it was a tight game. With just a few minutes left to play and the score very close, Todd Roberts made two free throws to put us back in the game, but the outstanding play — and the reason I remember Danny Shearer becoming an Oldham County hero — happened with the clock coming even closer to the end of the game. We were behind by one point. Danny Shearer dribbled, literally in circles, burning up time on the clock — and then with 38 seconds left on the clock he drove to the basket and made a layup, putting the Colonels ahead 43 to 42. We won!

When Danny hit the layup, over a thousand OCHS fans, and fans from other counties in our region, went crazy. I remember that exact moment now over 50 years later. We were going to win, and the finals were not that far away.

The only team in our way was Seneca High, which was the team favored to win the Sweet 16 that year. It did not matter. We were hot! The Colonels had never been this hot before and we were going to win.

As we prepared for the game with Seneca, the crowd driving to the games increased dramatically. Back in those days there were only three TV stations on the air in Louisville. So, everybody watched the same news and sports. The press loved the Colonels! We had come out of nowhere and now we were playing the number one ranked team in the state. The rumor was: whoever won this game, would win the state. The stakes could not be higher.

People from all over the region showed up to support the Colonels. We were an army of fans for the Cinderella Team! When we got to our seats at the game, the crowd was rocking. The cheerleaders had us on our feet and cheering! All of us. We were psyched! The Colonels are going to the finals and we are going to win!

The game started!

Seneca was favored to win. Mike Redd was on the Seneca team and he was already famous in Kentucky. There was talk that he was possibly the best high school basketball player ever in the state of Kentucky. Redd was not the only formidable foe. Another player on the Seneca team was Westley Unseld, who later played college ball and then became a top player in the NBA. He was the driving force in taking the Baltimore Bullets franchise to four NBA Finals, and won the championship in 1978 over the Seattle Super Sonics, in which he was named the Finals MVP. Unseld was inducted into the Naismith Memorial Basketball Hall of Fame in 1988 and in 1996, he was named as one of the NBA's 50 Greatest Players of all time.

Our boys were up against one of the greatest basketball players to ever set foot on a Kentucky high school gym floor. No problem. We were gonna win!

Our boys did great. The first period we kept Seneca off the scoreboard until the last seconds of the first period. We completely stole the show the first half of the game. According to *The Courier-Journal*, "Danny Shearer cemented his bid for all-tourney honors with some fabulous driving and fancy dribbling." I was in the crowd and we were on our feet the entire first half.

The teams went to the locker rooms with the score Seneca 19 - OCHS 17. The whisper had become a roar that we were going to win State for the first time ever! Everyone knew that Seneca was the only team that really stood between us and the championship, and even though they had these great players, our boys were kicking their ass!

We lost.

Seneca got itself together during the halftime break. The Colonels did their best, and we out-maneuvered Seneca on numerous occasions, but we simply could not make a basket to save our lives, or save our chances to be State Champs.

Seneca won, and they went on to beat Dunbar 72 to 66, and they became State Champs. Seneca also won the Mr. Basketball award that year with Mike Redd taking home the trophy. The following year, in 1964, Wes Unseld, the other great player that we had to compete with, won the Mr. Basketball award. Our boys had been up against some of the best high school players ever to set foot in Freedom Hall.

Danny won the All-State-Tourney player, the first OCHS player ever to win that award.

The Courier-Journal and the Louisville television stations were filled with stories about the Colonels — "The Cinderella Team."

Here is some of the press from *The Courier-Journal*:

"Cols Get Heroes' Welcome from State"

"A cavalcade of some 400 cars was on hand Sunday afternoon at Brownsboro Road Shopping Center to meet the Oldham County Colonels as they returned home after giving the 8th Region their strongest representation in 17 years...."

"The Colonels were escorted back to Oldham County High by the motorcade that traveled through Crestwood, Centerfield, Ballardsville and La Grange. They were met at the school by another large gathering and these plus those in the motorcade, approximately 1800 fans, met in the gymnasium where informal ceremonies were held honoring the team. ..."

"After the program fans filed by and shook the hands of the team and coaches. . . the meeting was summed up by Mr. Dick (Norman Dick) when he reminded the group of this year's slogan, 'WE IN '63' and stated that next year it would be 'MORE IN 64'."

I was one of the people in the cavalcade and at the gym. I do not specifically remember shaking all the players and coaches' hands, but I am sure I did. It was the first time ever that I been caught up in something so much larger than myself.

Back in the Sixties, Adolph Rupp, basketball coach at the University of Kentucky, was the king of basketball coaches — not just in Kentucky but nationwide. When Rupp talked, people listened. After the Sweet 16, Coach Rupp sent Oldham County Colonels Coach Barney Thweatt a letter, which was printed in *The Courier-Journal*:

Coach Barney Thweatt
Oldham County High School

Dear Coach:

Congratulations on the wonderful year you have had. I sat there during the State Tournament and was thrilled at the wonderfully play of your boys. You have turned in an outstanding coaching job and I wish you continued success.

Sincerely yours,

ADOLPH RUPP
University of Kentucky

We should not forget the cheerleaders. They did better than the boys at winning awards. The OCHS cheerleading squad won The Kentucky Association of PEP Organization Sponsors runner-up trophy for being the best pepsters at the state tournament.

The 1963 Kentucky High School Basketball Tournament had been "Our Moment." The glow from that moment lasted for months, and we started preparing for "More in 64." They started free basketball clinics at the OCHS Gym on Saturday mornings. I remember going to those clinics. They were early on Saturday mornings, but I did not complain. Head coach Ray Warmath and his assistants would be at the gym when we got there. Sometimes there were 30 or 40 kids from all over the county. A station wagon would show up with 3 or 4 kids from Liberty. Another load of kids from Crestwood would arrive. Then more and more.

Our primary focus was practicing the drills: how to pass and dribble; how to set a pick. We practiced layups. We did laps around the inside of the gym. Lap after lap after lap. We did some shooting, but mostly we worked on the skill-drills. Our coaches wanted us to grow up knowing how to pass and dribble without thinking about it. Our coaches, mothers, and fathers were training the next generation of OCHS basketball players and they were serious about it. The county was psyched for "More in '64." Now that we knew that we could do it, the more we wanted it.

And then one day everything changed in America.

President Kennedy was assassinated. It was the beginning of the Sixties in America and there was no going back. This was the beginning of the change, and for those of us who lived through that era, it was the beginning of pain, fear and confusion — happening so fast and deep in our being that a decade later the entire world had changed completely.

As for me, I continued going to basketball clinics the fall of 1963. However, when the "More in '64" season started coming around, I started watching something else on TV. I became infatuated with the Winter Olympics taking place in Innsbruck, Austria, and Scott changed forever. I watched Jimmy Huega, Billy Kidd and Buddy Werner ski in those Olympics and I did not want to play basketball anymore. I wanted to learn how to ski. And I did learn how to ski. It became my passion.

I now live in Colorado and I am still skiing.

Danny continued to play basketball. He and I eventually went to the same college: Georgetown College in Georgetown, KY. He was a star there just like he was a star at OCHS. I am not surprised. Georgetown played the kind of basketball Danny loved — fast basketball, emphasizing speed and skill over height. There, a short guy like Danny could play circles around the big guys if he had the skills. Danny did. I believe he won numerous awards and trophies while playing for the Georgetown Tigers.

I believe he played at Georgetown before the word "dunk" had ever been used in basketball. When you mentioned dunking back then you were talking about a doughnut in your coffee. America is not the only thing that changed. Basketball in America has completely changed since Danny played.

Then the other Kennedy was killed. Martin Luther King was killed. Over 56,000 American soldiers were killed in Vietnam. Two to four million Vietnamese were killed during "The American War". Woodstock, Kent State. Then Nixon resigned. And that was just the news up to 1974. It had been only a little over a decade that OCHS had been psyched to "win State" in 1963.

America kept changing fast, for at least another decade. The end of the "60's" was also the end of my hearing about Danny. I lost track of Danny until my Dad mentioned him in 1991. And then Danny died in 2000. Apparently, he'd lived in Madison, Indiana, and according to his obituary, he died in an accident of some sort.

America changed so much, so fast! The world Danny knew as "Mr. Basketball" had simply disappeared. Maybe he wondered if that time had even happened at all. I suspect he was just like the rest of us who felt that the America we grew up in was now barely recognizable.

Danny was always someone I wished I'd known — or at least met — as an adult. I wanted to shake his hand and tell him how much I admired him, that, in fact, a whole town, a whole county — loved him. I'd like to have told him that he was our hero, that for all of us who knew him while he played for us, he had been our "Mr. Basketball," just like the "Cinderella Colonels" were our team — a bunch of small-town kids from Oldham County who went to the big city and kicked ass for us. They did what had never been done before and they were our small-town heroes.

Against all odds they went to State, and for the first half of the Seneca game, the Colonels were playing and beating the best high school team in Kentucky. And for that first half of the Seneca game there was no team better in the State of Kentucky than the Oldham County

Colonels. And, of course, if you are the best high school basketball team in Kentucky then you are also probably the best basketball team in America, and for the first half of a semifinal game in Louisville, Kentucky our boys were the best in America.

At least that is the way I tell the story.

THANK YOU:

The Cinderella Team: Todd Roberts, #33; Gary Chisholm, #11; Keith Oglesby, #45; Ronnie Webster, #52; David Prather, #41; Billy Brown, #34; Harry Westmoreland, #53; Pete Wright, #31; Jackie Swann, #10; Billy Mathis, #44; Bobby Jenkins, #21; Norman Brown, #51; Eddie Wilhoyte, #54; and Danny Shearer, #00.

OCHS CHEERLEADING SQUAD FOR 1963: Sara Roberts, Elaine Hargrove, Joan Theiss, Susan Whitfield, Mae Woolum, Joyce Bell. and Helen Magers.

COACHING STAFF: Coach Barney Thweatt and Assistant Coach Ray Warmath.

MANAGERS for the TEAM: Roger Cranfill, Larry Cranfill, Mike Boyles, and John Bowman.

Danny's number when he played for Oldham County High School was 00. My high school retired the number

00 out of respect for Danny Shearer after he was named our "Mr. Basketball."

Epilogue

I moved from LA to Boston in the early 80s. Shortly after I moved to "the big city" Bruce Springsteen put out a song called "My Home Town." The song literally stops me in my tracks. It does not matter if I hear the song in a bar in Harvard Square in 1984 or a restaurant in Vail in 2017, his description of his Home Town is so powerful – it hurts. He loved his home town and I loved growing up in La Grange. I miss it.

When I go there now, I walk the streets and remember the buildings as I knew them as a child. The name "The View from Karen's Book Barn" is not an accident. Jones and Shearer – Danny Shearer's mom's store was directly across the street from the Book Barn. *The Oldham Era* was a few doors down and Donnie Ireland's dad worked in Gatewood Drugs, which is either next door to the Book Barn or used to be in the building that the Book Barn was located in. Head's Drugs is just down the block and the streets of La Grange that Donnie used to walk in the late hours of night are still here. These buildings, streets, and the people that occupied them were my world in my childhood and high school years.

I recently visited an ole LA friend that is now in her 90s. She used to be my Cub Scout leader when I was a child and we both discussed how lucky we are that the "Old La Grange" is still there. Now LA has become a tourist attraction and probably they will keep the downtown intact for at least another decade or so. With the buildings, comes the memories of those that lived and worked in them.

Another piece of music that captured the essence of LA is John Cougar Mellencamp's song, "Small Town." His words "I live in a small town, where there's little opportunity." There are a couple of reasons why I left La Grange/Kentucky in 1983 but certainly at the top of the list was the fact that my future was in those big cities of the northeast, Colorado, and Europe. And, just like southerners have been doing for over a century, I moved north to find work and a new life. And just like my southern ancestors, as I worked in the north, I dreamed of my home that I left. In that same Mellencamp song, John makes a simple prophecy. He says, "Gonna die in this small town; and that's prob'ly where they'll bury me." He's right. I will probably be buried in La Grange, my home town. I hope you enjoyed the book!

Acknowledgements

Well, at the top of the list I have to thank Karen Eldridge, the owner of Karen's Book Barn. Thanks for opening the Book Barn – a great place to read, drink coffee, chat with friends, and wake up in the morning. Also, thank you Karen for letting my use the name of your store in my book.

I would not be writing books if not for Mary Johnson. She and I have been radical political allies since the late 70s and when it came time to put out my first book, she held my hand, told me what to do, and how to do it. She is still holding my hand and telling me what to do and how to do it. The result – another book! Thank you, Mary!

Now, I have to thank the long list of good friends that have critiqued my work and helped me edit my stories. They include: Anne Conkin, Buddha Hildenbrandt, Merryl Gibbs, Lise Neer, Ellen Prager, Lucy Radcliff, Judy De Tar, Pushy Galore, and Barbara Manley Calloway for her fantastic photographs of LA!

Last, but not least, I need to thank Winnie, my biggest fan! Winnie Hepler has always encouraged me to write. She liked my style of writing and the subjects I chose to write about. She read just about everything I wrote and her editorial comments were always on point. Winnie pasted away back in the beginning of the year. However, before she left us, she did read "The View" – several times and always said to me, "The people of La Grange will like your book." I hope she is right.

About the Author

Author Scott Houchin sitting in front of Karen's Book Barn, La Grange, Ky. *PHOTO: Barbara Manley Calloway.*

Scott Houchin is a writer and "local" from La Grange Kentucky. He has lived all over America: the big cities of New England; the snow country of Colorado; the mountains of Tennessee; and now he shares residency in the desert of Arizona and his home state of Kentucky.

Prior to being a writer, Scott was a political activist and federal employee who worked environmental, peace, and civil rights issues for the last 35 years before retiring. Now he fills his time writing books, cross country skiing, hiking, and bicycling all over North America and Europe.

Made in the USA
Columbia, SC
18 May 2021